Contrasts

A Parallel between the Noble Edifices of the Fourteenth and the Fifteenth Centuries, and Similar Buildings of the Present Day; Shewing the Present Decay of Taste: Accompanied by Appropriate Cert.

Augustus Welby Northmore Pugin

Copyright © 2016

All rights reserved.

ISBN: 1523814470
ISBN-13: 978-1523814473

Table of Contents

PREFACE 6

CONTRASTS; OR, A PARALLEL BETWEEN THE NOBLE EDIFICES OF THE XIVTH AND XVTH CENTURIES, AND SIMILAR BUILDINGS OF THE PRESENT DAY.................. 8

CHAPTER I ON THE FEELINGS WHICH PRODUCED THE GREAT EDIFICES OF THE MIDDLE AGES. 8

CHAPTER II ON THE STATE OF ARCHITECTURE IN ENGLAND IMMEDIATELY PRECEDING THE CHANGE OF RELIGION. 11

CHAPTER III OF THE PILLAGE AND DESTRUCTION OF THE CHURCHES UNDER HENRY THE EIGHTH. 13

CHAPTER IV ON THE RAVAGES AND DESTRUCTION THE CHURCHES SUFFERED UNDER EDWARD VI., AND AFTER THE FINAL ESTABLISHMENT OF THE NEW RELIGION 18

CHAPTER V ON THE PRESENT DEGRADED STATE OF ECCLESIASTICAL BUILDINGS... 25

CONCLUSION ON THE WRETCHED STATE OF ARCHITECTURE AT THE PRESENT DAY. 37

APPENDIX... 44

WORKS DESIGNED AND ETCHED BY A. WELBY PUGIN, ARCHITECT.. 59

Augustus Welby Northmore Pugin

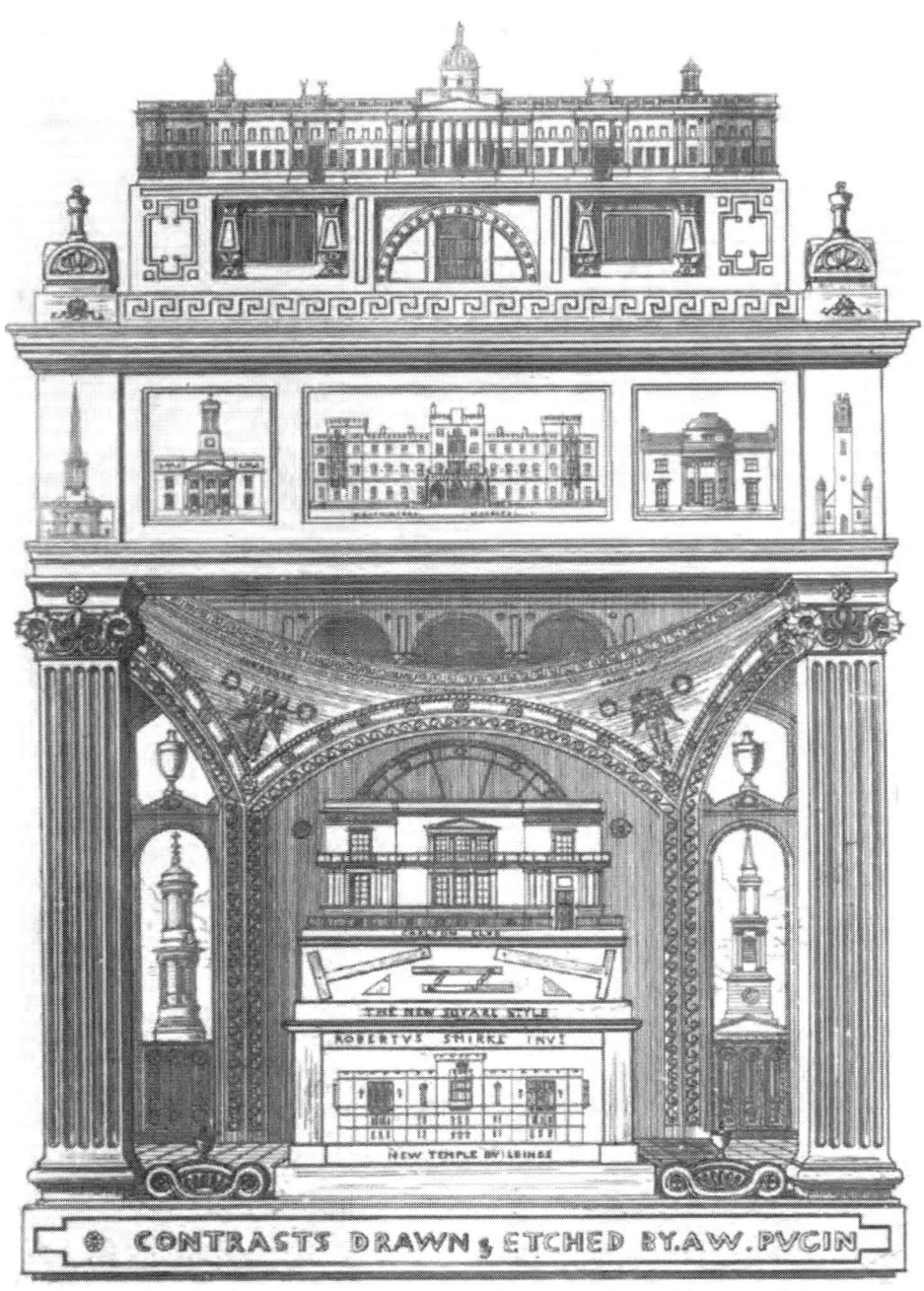

SELECTIONS FROM THE WORKS OF VARIOUS CELEBRATED BRITISH ARCHITECTS

Augustus Welby Northmore Pugin

𝕮𝖔𝖓𝖙𝖗𝖆𝖘𝖙𝖘;

OR,

A PARALLEL BETWEEN THE NOBLE EDIFICES

OF THE FOURTEENTH AND FIFTEENTH CENTURIES,

AND

SIMILAR BUILDINGS OF THE PRESENT DAY;

SHEWING

THE PRESENT DECAY OF TASTE:

𝔄𝔠𝔠𝔬𝔪𝔭𝔞𝔫𝔦𝔢𝔡 𝔟𝔶 𝔞𝔭𝔭𝔯𝔬𝔭𝔯𝔦𝔞𝔱𝔢 𝔗𝔢𝔵𝔱.

By A. WELBY PUGIN, Architect.

LONDON:

PRINTED FOR THE AUTHOR,

AND PUBLISHED BY HIM, AT ST. MARIE'S GRANGE,

NEAR SALISBURY, WILTS.

M.DCCC.XXXVI.

Contrasts

PREFACE

In presenting this Volume to the Public, I trust that the feelings which have induced me to undertake its publication will be duly understood; and that it will not be imagined I have acted from any private feelings towards those modern Professors of Architecture, whose Works I have placed in comparison with similar Edifices of a more ancient period.

I hope it will be acknowledged that I have conducted the comparison with the greatest candour; and, in selecting the Works of the leading men of the day, I have placed the architectural productions of the Nineteenth Century in fair contrast with those of the Fourteenth and Fifteenth. That the former Edifices appear to great disadvantage, when thus tried by the scale of real excellence, will be readily admitted by all who are competent to think on the subject: and I hope this Work will prove how little title this Age has to one of improvement on the score of architectural excellence, when, in truth, that science is at a very low ebb: in which state, I fear, it will remain, unless the same feelings which influenced the old designers in the composition of their Works, can be restored:-a result which, though I most fervently wish, I dare not at present hope for. But I feel thoroughly convinced, that it is only by similar glorious feelings that similar glorious results can be obtained.

I am well aware that the sentiments I have expressed in this Work are but little suited to the taste and opinions of the Age in which we live: by a vast number they will be received with ridicule, and, by some, considered as the result of a heated imagination. To these I answer, they are not the result of a sudden and momentary impression, but have been produced by continued study and deep reflection on the noble Works of the Middle

Ages. And those, who will accompany me through the following pages, may, perhaps, be convinced that there is more truth in the position I have taken, than they were, at first, willing to allow me.

A. WELBY PUGIN

ST. MARIE'S GRANGE, near SALISBURY, May, 1836.

CONTRASTS; OR, A PARALLEL BETWEEN THE NOBLE EDIFICES OF THE XIVTH AND XVTH CENTURIES, AND SIMILAR BUILDINGS OF THE PRESENT DAY

CHAPTER I
ON THE FEELINGS WHICH PRODUCED THE GREAT EDIFICES OF THE MIDDLE AGES.

On comparing the Architectural Works of the present Century with those of the Middle Ages, the wonderful superiority of the latter must strike every attentive observer; and the mind is naturally led to reflect on the causes which have wrought this mighty change, and to endeavour to trace the fall of Architectural taste, from the period of its first decline in this country to the present day; and this will form the subject of the following pages.
It will be readily admitted that the great test of Architectural beauty is the fitness of the design to the purpose for which it is intended, and that the style of a building should so correspond with its use that the spectator may at once perceive the purpose for which it was erected.
Acting on this principle, different nations have given birth to so many various styles of Architecture, each suited to their climate, customs, and religion; and as it is among edifices of this latter class that we look for the most splendid and lasting monuments, there can be but little doubt that the religious ideas and ceremonies of these different people had by far the

greatest influence in the formation of their various styles of Architecture. The more closely we compare the temples of the Pagan nations with their religious rites and mythologies, the more shall we be satisfied with the truth of this assertion.

But who can regard those stupendous Ecclesiastical Edifices of the Middle Ages (the more special objects of this work), without feeling this observation in its full force? Here every portion of the sacred fabric bespeaks its origin; the very plan of the edifice is the emblem of human redemption-each portion is destined for the performance of some solemn rite of the Christian church. Here is the brazen font where the waters of baptism wash away the stain of original sin; there stands the gigantic pulpit, from which the sacred truths and ordinances are from time to time proclaimed to the congregated people; behold yonder, resplendent with precious gems, is the high altar, the seat of the most holy mysteries, and the tabernacle of the Highest! It is, indeed, a sacred place; and well does the fabric bespeak its destined purpose: the eye is carried up and lost in the height of the vaulting and the intricacy of the ailes; the rich and varied hues of the stained windows, the modulated light, the gleam of the tapers, the richness of the altars, the venerable images of the departed just,-all alike conspire to fill the mind with veneration for the place, and to make it feel the sublimity of Christian worship. And when the deep intonations of the bells from the lofty campaniles, which summon the people to the house of prayer, have ceased, and the solemn chant of the choir swells through the vast edifice,-cold, indeed, must be the heart of that mall who does not cry out with the Psalmist,

Domine dilixi decorem domus tuæ, et locum habitationis gloriæ tuæ.

Such effects as these can only be produced on the mind by buildings, the composition of which has emanated from men who were thoroughly embued with devotion for. and faith in, the religion for whose worship they were erected.

Their whole energies were directed towards attaining excellence; they were actuated by far nobler motives than the hopes of pecuniary reward, or even the applause and admiration of mankind. They felt they were engaged in the most glorious occupation that can fall to the lot of man, that of raising a temple to the worship of the true and living God.

It was this feeling that operated alike on the master mind that planned the edifice, and on the patient sculptor whose chisel wrought each varied and beautiful detail. It was this feeling that induced the ancient masons, in spite of labour, danger, and difficulties, to persevere till they had raised their gigantic spires into the very regions of the clouds. It was this feeling that induced the ecclesiastics of old to devote their revenues to this pious purpose, and to labour with their own hands in the accomplishment of the work; and it is a feeling that may be traced throughout the whole of the numerous edifices of the middle ages, and which, amidst the great variety of genius which their varied styles display, still bespeak the unity of purpose which influenced their builders and artists.

They borrowed their ideas from no. heathen rites, nor sought for decorations from the idolatrous emblems of a strange people. The foundation and progress of the Christian faith, and the sacraments and ceremonies of the church, formed an ample and noble field for the exercise of their talents; and it is an incontrovertible fact, that every class of artists who flourished during those glorious periods selected their subjects from this inexhaustible source, and devoted their greatest efforts towards the embellishment of ecclesiastical edifices.

Yes, it was, indeed, the faith, the zeal, and, above all, the unity, of our ancestors, that enabled them to conceive and raise those wonderful fabrics that still remain to excite our wonder and admiration. They were erected for the most solemn rites of Christian worship, when the term Christian had but one signification throughout the world; when the glory of the house of God formed an important consideration with mankind, when men were zealous for religion, liberal in their gifts, and devoted to her cause; they were erected ere heresy had destroyed faith, schism had put an end to unity, and avarice had instigated the plunder of that wealth that had been consecrated to the service of the church. When these feelings entered in, the spell was broken, the Architecture itself fell with the religion to which it owed its birth, and was succeeded by a mixed and base style devoid of science or elegance, which was rapidly followed by others, till at length, regulated by no system, devoid of unity, but made to suit the ideas and means of each sect as they sprung up, buildings for religious worship present as great incongruities, varieties, and extravagances, as the sects and ideas which have emanated from the new religion which first wrought this great change. In order to prove the truth of these assertions, I will proceed, first, to shew the state of Architecture in this country immediately before the great change of religion; secondly, the fatal effects produced by that change on Architecture; and, thirdly, .the present degraded state of Architectural taste, and the utter want of those feelings which alone can restore Architecture to its ancient noble position.

CHAPTER II
ON THE STATE OF ARCHITECTURE IN ENGLAND IMMEDIATELY PRECEDING THE CHANGE OF RELIGION.

At the period I am about to enter upon, Architecture had attained a most extraordinary degree of excellence in this country.

The splendid Chapels of King's College, Cambridge, St. George at Windsor, and Henry the Seventh at Westminster, are alone sufficient to attest the fact; the stone ceiling of the latter being a complete masterpiece of bold and elegant construction. Many extensive and beautiful Collegiate buildings, such as Magdalen, All Souls, Jesus, Eton, and Christ's Church, were rapidly advancing towards completion; and most of the parochial churches received extensive I repairs and important additions, and many were entirely rebuilt at this era, 80 prolific in elegant erections.

The religious houses also kept pace with the general feeling for noble buildings: Bath Abbey was erected by Prior Bird; great works were carrying on at the large Abbeys of Reading, Glastonbury, and St. Alban's; and, indeed, there are hardly any remains of monastic buildings in existence, some portions of which cannot be ascribed to this era. At the same time so many magnificent ecclesiastical edifices were thus in progress, several palaces and castellated mansions were erecting in a style of splendour and convenience that greatly surpassed all previous buildings of this description. The palaces of Richmond, Greenwich, Hampton Court, and Nonsuch, and the noble residences of Thombury Castle, East Barsham House, Oxburgh Hall, Cowdry House, and a host of others equally fine, were all of this date. Their style was imposing, rich, and purely of a domestic character, and every portion of exterior ornament and internal decoration was executed in the most perfect manner. Joiners' work and wood carving had, indeed, attained a degree of excellence previously unknown; and all descriptions of chasing and metal ornaments were executed with a delicacy, taste, and sentiment, that has never since been equalled.

The art of glass painting and enamelling had also arrived at its greatest perfection; and the miniatures and illuminations of manuscripts of this period are deserving of the highest admiration, both for the purity of drawing and the brilliancy and arrangement of the colours. To produce so much excellence, and such a multiplicity of great works all nearly coeval, we must naturally conclude that able directors and skilful operatives abounded in every department of the building art; and it is a curious fact, that, notwithstanding the great variety of form and ornament employed at this epoch, we may easily trace the unity of ideas and principles that pervaded and influenced their designs; so that we are able, without hesitation, to ascribe the date to their erections, from barely inspecting the edifices.

Here, therefore, on the eve of the great change of religion, we find Architecture in a high state of perfection, both as regards design and execution; we find it proceeding with activity and unity to the eleventh hour, insomuch that, when the blow was struck, many great edifices were in a state of progress, and the unfinished condition in which we still see them is entirely owing to the great change which at once prevented their completion, and destroyed those sentiments which had prompted their foundation.

Having thus briefly noticed the state of Architecture previous to the change of religion, I will now proceed to describe its condition afterwards, during the latter part of the reign of Henry VIII., and the succeeding ones of Edward VI. and Elizabeth.

CHAPTER III
OF THE PILLAGE AND DESTRUCTION OF THE CHURCHES UNDER HENRY THE EIGHTH.

> I sing the deeds of great King Harry,
> Of Ned his son, and daughter Mary;
> The old religion's alteration,
> And Church of England's first foundation;
> And how the King became its head;
> How Abbeys fell, what blood was shed;
> Of rapine, sacrilege, and theft,
> And Church of gold and land bereft.

I have now arrived at a most important era in religion, as well as the architecture of this country; and, by carefully comparing the decay of the latter with the changes successively made in the former, I trust I shall be enabled clearly to shew the intimate connexion between the two, which I asserted at the commencement of this treatise.

The origin of what is usually termed the Reformation in this country, is too well known to need much dilating upon; but it will be necessary to say a few words on the subject, to enable the reader to follow up the comparison I have in view.

King Henry the Eighth, finding all the hopes he had conceived of the Pontiff's acquiescence in his unlawful divorce totally at an end, determined to free himself from all spiritual restraint of the Apostolic see; and, for that purpose, caused himself to be proclaimed supreme head of the English church. This arrogant and impious step drew forth the indignation of those who had the constancy and firmness to prefer the interests of religion to the will of a tyrant, and who boldly represented the injustice and impiety of a layman pretending to be the supreme head of a Christian church.

Their opposition was, however, fruitless, and a bitter persecution was commenced against those who had boldly resisted this dangerous and novel innovation; and amongst the numerous victims who suffered on this occasion, the names of those learned and pious men, Bishop Fisher, Thomas More, and Abbot Whiting, need only be cited to shew the injustice and cruelty of this merciless tyrant.

The king, however, now established in his new dignity, by dint of rewards to those who were base enough to truckle to his will, and axe and halter to any who dared withstand his usurpations, found it necessary to find some means to replenish his coffers, and to secure the assistance he might require in the furtherance of his sacrilegious projects.

The step he took on this occasion, proved the total overthrow of art, and paved the way for all those disasterous events that so rapidly afterwards succeeded each other.

Ever since the first conversion of this country to the Christian faith, pious and munificent individuals had always been found zealous to establish and endow a vast number of religious houses; to the labours of whose inmates we are indebted not only for the preservation and advancement of literature and science, but even for the conception and partial execution both of the great ecclesiastical buildings themselves, and the exquisite and precious ornaments with which they were filled.

By the unwearied zeal and industry of these men, thus relieved from all worldly cares, and so enabled to devote their lives to the study of all that was sublime and admirable, their churches rose in gigantic splendour; their almonries and sacristies were filled with sacred vessels and sumptuous vestments, the precious materials of which were only exceeded by the exquisite forms into which they had been wrought; while the shelves of their libraries groaned under a host of ponderous volumes, the least of which required years of intense and unceasing application for its production.

It would be an endless theme to dilate on all the advantages accruing from these splendid establishments; suffice it to observe, that it was through their boundless charity and hospitality the poor were entirely maintained.

They formed alike the places for the instruction of youth, and the quiet retreat of a mature age; and the vast results that the monastic bodies have produced, in all classes of art and science, shew the excellent use they made of that time which was not consecrated to devotion and the immediate duties of their orders.

To a monarch, however, who neither respected sanctity or art, these institutions only offered a lure to his avarice, and the sure means of replenishing his exhausted treasury; and, regardless of the consequences of so sacrilegious a step, he proceeded to exercise the power of his newly acquired headship, and to devote to his own use and purposes those lands which ancient piety had dedicated to God, and which had been the support of the religious, the learned, and the poor, for so many centuries.

He accomplished this great change in the most artful manner, by instituting commissioners for the pretended reformation of ecclesiastical abuses; but, in reality, to accomplish the entire overthrow of the religious houses, by forging accusations of irregularity against them[1], and by executing those who opposed his intentions, on the score of denying his supremacy[2].

By such means, he obtained an act of parliament, for the suppression, to his use, of all those houses whose revenues were 300 marks a-year, and under.

Monstrous as this measure was, by which 376 conventual establishments were dissolved, and an immense number of religious persons scattered abroad, it was only intended as a prelude to one which soon followed, and which was no less than the entire suppression of all the larger abbeys, and a great number of colleges, hospitals, and free chapels: of which Baker, in his "Chronicle," computes the number to have been, of monasteries, 6405; colleges, 90; 100 hospitals for poor men; and chantries and free chapels, 2374. The whole of whose lands, together with an immense treasure of ecclesiastical ornaments, of every description, were appropriated, by this rapacious and sacrilegious tyrant, to his own use, and the rightful possessors left utterly destitute.

This measure may be considered as a fatal blow to the progress of Architecture; and, from this period, we have only to trace a melancholy series of destructions and mutilations, by which the most glorious edifices of the Middle Ages have either been entirely demolished, or so shorn of their original beauties, that what remains only serves to awaken our regret at what is for ever lost to us.

On the slaughter and dispersion of the religious, all the buildings then in progress were, of course, immediately stopped; a vast number of their former inmates fled, to obtain an asylum in some foreign land, where yet

---

[1] See Appendix, A.

[2] See Appendix, B.

the ancient faith remained inviolate; those who remained, reduced to indigence, became the humble suitors for that charity they had so often liberally bestowed on others; and with bleeding hearts, and bitter lamentations, they beheld those edifices, on which they had bestowed so much labour and consideration, consigned to rapacious court parasites, as the reward of some grovelling submission, or in the chance of play[3].

They beheld the lead tom from the roofs and spires of their venerable churches, to satisfy the wasteful extravagance of a profligate court; and those beauteous and precious ornaments, which had enshrined the relics of the departed saints, or served for centuries in the most solemn rites of the church, sink in mere masses of metal, under the fire of the crucible.

Their libraries pillaged, their archives destroyed; the very remains of their illustrious dead torn from their tombs, and treated with barbarous indignity.

So suddenly had all this been brought to pass, that many buildings were hurled down, ere the cement, with which they were erected, had hardened with time; and p1any a mason, by the unwearied strokes of whose chisel some beautiful form had been wrought, lived to see the result of his labours mutilated, by the axes of the destroyer[4].

The effect of such scenes as these, on the minds of those clergy who still remained in cathedral and other churches, may easily be conceived. Apprehensive of a similar fate to that which had fallen on their monastic brethren, they remained paralysed; and no further efforts were made at beautifying those edifices they so soon expected would be plundered: and they waited, in dreadful suspense, the next step the sacrilegious tyrant would take, when either his avarice or his necessities would lead him to it.

It is a very common error to suppose that the change of religion, in this country, was the result of popular feeling, and carried by a coup de main: the truth, is, the great fabric of the church was undermined, by slow degrees, one step producing another, till, like all revolutions, it far exceeded the intentions of its first advocates; and I do believe that, had Henry himself foreseen the full extent to which his first impious step would lead, he would have been deterred by the dreadful prospect from proceeding in his career. Certain it is, he was the father of persecution against the tenets of the Protestant religion in this country[5].

---

[3] See Appendix, C.

[4] See Appendix, D.

[5] See Appendix, E.

By his six articles, he confirmed all the leading tenets of the Catholic faith[6]; and, indeed, the only alteration he made in the mass itself was, erasing the prayer for the pope, and the name of St. Thomas a Becket, from the missals. In fine, images were retained in churches, the sacrifice of the mass every where offered up, in the usual manner, and the rites of the old religion performed, with only this difference, that their splendour was greatly reduced, in consequence of the king having appropriated all the richest ecclesiastical ornaments to his own use.

It is impossible, therefore, that Henry can be, by any means, ranked among the number of what are termed Reformers, except so far as his disposition to plunder and demolition, feelings so congenial to that body, will entitle him to fellowship with them; for, indeed, in no other respects was he at all similar to those who proceeded afterwards on the foundation he had laid. He had foolishly imagined, he should have been able to seize the church's wealth and power into his own hands, and preserve the same unity and discipline as those who held it by apostolic right; but grievously was he disappointed.

The suppression of the religious houses, and the spoliation and desecration of those shrines and places which had so long been considered sacred, had raised doubts and uncertainties among men which were more easily excited than suppressed.

The promiscuous use of the Holy Scriptures[7] and various heretical works imported from Germany, had produced feelings of irreverence for the clergy. and contempt for religion, which was increased by the innovations they beheld daily made by those in power, on the rights and property of ecclesiastics; and Henry lived to perceive and deplore, that neither his fagots nor his halters could preserve any thing like unity of creed; but that, the great spell being broken which had so long kept men together. they were as little disposed to be restrained by rules prescribed by him, as he had been by those of the ancient faith from which he had departed.

During his life, however, the cathedral and parochial churches suffered little, except being despoiled of their richest ornaments, all the destruction having fallen on the monastic edifices; nor was it till his infant son, Edward VI., ascended the throne, that the full fanaticism and feelings of the new religion were displayed, or the work of robbery and destruction fully commenced.

---

[6] See Appendix, F.

[7] See Appendix, G.

CHAPTER IV
ON THE RAVAGES AND DESTRUCTION THE CHURCHES SUFFERED UNDER EDWARD VI., AND AFTER THE FINAL ESTABLISHMENT OF THE NEW RELIGION

> Here altar cloaths lie scattered, and
> There does a broken altar stand;
> Some steal away the crucifix;
> And some the silver candlesticks;
> Rich vestments others do convey,
> And antipendiums bear away;
> And what they thought not fit to steal,
> They burn as an effect of zeal.
>
> *Ward's Reformation.*

Disastrous as the latter part of Henry's reign proved to religion and ecclesiastical architecture, the succeeding one of Edward VI. was doubly so.

The church in this country had then for its supreme head a boy of nine years of age, incapable, of course, of either thinking or acting for himself, and fit only to be used as a mere machine, by those who actually constituted the government.

These consisted, unhappily, of men who considered church property in no other light than that of a legitimate source of plunder, and who, fearing that, should the ancient religion be restored, they would not only lose all chance of further enriching themselves, but might even be compelled to restore that which they had so iniquitously obtained, resolved on forming a new religion, dependant wholly on the temporal power, under colour of which they might pillage with impunity; and by abolishing all the grand and noble accompaniments which had, for so many centuries, rendered the sacred rites of religion so solemn and imposing, secure to their own use all these ornaments which served for those purposes, reduce a large portion of the clergy, and even demolish vast parts of the fabrics themselves, either to avail themselves of the materials, or benefit by their sale.

In order to accomplish these ends, those of the old bishops who would not consent to the impoverishment of their sees were displaced, and their bishoprics fined by men who were willing to surrender large portions of their temporalities to those in power[8], in order to obtain a dignity to which they had no legitimate right, and almost as little reasonable expectation of ever possessing.

The perfidious and dissembling Cranmer, who during the lifetime of Henry had outwardly conformed to the old system, now threw off the mask, declared himself a bitter enemy to what he had professed all his life, and, in order to ingratiate himself with the favourites of the day, was base enough to surrender into their hands half the lands belonging to the See of Canterbury.

All the church lands were every where reduced in a similar manner, and appropriated to the aggrandisement of the nobilities' estates; nor were the spoliations by any means confined to landed ecclesiastical property: for the protector, Somerset. having conceived the design of erecting a sumptuous mansion in the Strand, caused the demolition of the magnificent cloisters of St. Paul's, the nave of St. Bartholomew's priory church in Smith field (which had just been completed), five churches, and three bishops' palaces, for materials so little veneration for religion or art did these new churchmen profess. Nor, after this, can further proof he wanting to shew the total absence of all respect for buildings dedicated to religious worship, when the lord protector, who was actually the supreme head of the English church, demolishes large portions of the metropolitan cathedral, and a host of ecclesiastical edifices, to gratify a mere vain whim of his own[9].

To carry on this work of devastation and robbery, under the cover of restoring primitive simplicity and abolishing superstition, acts were passed

---

[8] See Appendix, H.

[9] See Appendix, I.

for defacing images, pulling down altars, and seizing on all those ecclesiastical ornaments which had escaped the rapacious hands of Henry's commissioners, or which had been suffered to remain as being absolutely necessary to perform the rites in the ancient manner; and so effectually were the churches now cleared out, that only one chalice and paten were suffered to remain in each[10]. The compilers of the new liturgy took infinite pains that none of their rites and ceremonies should either be irksome or expensive, or that they should impede in any way the plunder that was going on by introducing the use of any thing valuable or imposing. In fact, from the moment the new religion was established, all the great Architectural Edifices ceased to be of any real utility; the new rites could equally well have been performed in a capacious barn, only the policy of these churchmakers caused them to leave a few of the buildings, and retain a set of nominal dignitaries, in order to secure the lands and oblations which, without some such show, they thought it would be impossible to retain and collect. It is to this feeling of policy alone that we are indebted for the preservation of those cathedrals we now see: do not imagine, reader, it was the wonders of their construction or the elegance of their design that operated with these reformers for their preservation. It was not the loftiness of Salisbury's spire, the vastness of Ely's lantern, the lightness of Gloucester's choir, or the solemn grandeur of Wykeham's nave at Winchester, that caused them to be singled out and spared in the general havoc. There are mouldering remains scattered over the face of this country which mark the spots where once, in gigantic splendour, stood churches equally vast, equally fine, with those we now behold. Glastonbury, Crowland, Reading, St. Edmund's, and many others, were not inferior to any in scale or grandeur; they contained tombs of illustrious dead, shrines, chapels, all replete with works of wondrous skill. But they are gone; condemned to ruin and neglect, they perished piecemeal, and all that now remains of their once glorious piles are some unshapen masses of masonry, too firmly cemented to render their demolition lucrative.

And in a similar state should we now behold the cathedrals, had it not been arranged to keep just as much of the old system as would serve for the professors of the new; for these reformers, although they professed to revive the simplicity of the Apostles in all such matters, the continuation of which entailed expense or irksome duty on them, were quite unwilling to become imitators of their poverty. No, that was another question; they did not quarrel with the popish names of dean, canon, or prebend, because good incomes were attached to them, although I never heard of any of

---

[10] See Appendix, J.

these dignitaries being mentioned in Holy Writ, which to persons utterly rejecting the tradition of the church ought to have proved an insuperable objection. But an altar, which with its daily lighting and decoration entailed a considerable expense, and as its rich appendages formed no inconsiderable plunder, it is condemned to be pulled down, and a common square table set in its place, as being, forsooth, more agreeable to apostolic use. Why did not these restorers of simplicity fly the churches, and muster in an upper chamber? because then they must have renounced all pretensions to the lands; and so they' sat down content in the same stalls, and in the same choir as that which had so lately been occupied by their Catholic predecessors.

This is only one among the many inconsistencies that attended the establishment of the new church; and I only mention it to shew, from what base and sordid motives we are indebted for the partial preservation of what remains, and how little any feelings, except those of interest and expediency, had any part in it. I have hitherto described the dreadful results which were produced on the buildings by the combined ravages of avarice and fanaticism; I will now proceed to shew how materially they continued to suffer, when the new religion was, finally, by law established.

The altars had every where been demolished; the stained windows dashed from the mullions they had so brilliantly filled; the images of the saints left headless in their mutilated niches, or utterly defaced; the cross, that great emblem of human redemption, every where trampled under foot; the carved work broken down; the tabernacles destroyed ; and the fabrics denuded, as far as possible, of those appearances which would announce them as having been devoted to the celebration of the solemn offices of the ancient church, and left as bare as the strictest disciple of the Genevan church could desire.

Plunder was likewise nearly over; all that was rich and valuable had long disappeared; even brass was becoming scarce; and the leaden coffins of the dead had been so exhausted, they could but rarely be found to supply the melting-pot[11].

Further excesses were forbid; the buildings were declared to be sufficiently purified of ancient superstition; the axe and the hammer are laid by; and the shattered edifices are ordained to undergo a second ordeal, almost as destructive as the first, in being fitted up for the new form of worship: and, when we reflect on the horrible repairs, alterations, and demolitions, that have taken place in our venerable edifices, ever directed by a tepid and parsimonious clergy, brutal and jobbing parochial authorities,

---

[11] See Appendix, K.

and ignorant and tasteless operatives. I do not hesitate to say, that the lover of ancient art has more to regret, during the period the present establishment has had the churches in possession, than even during the fatal period that drove the ancient churchmen from them.

The manner of preparing the churches for the exercise of the new liturgy, consisted in blocking up the nave and aisles with dozing-pens, termed pews; above this mass of partitions rose a rostrum, for the preacher, reader, and his respondent; whilst a square table, surmounted by the king's arms, which had every where replaced the crucified Redeemer, conclude the list of necessary erections, which, I need hardly say, were as unsightly as the ancient arrangements were appropriate and beautiful.

Had propriety and fitness been considered, instead of economy, the old churches would have been abandoned altogether, and places of worship erected very similar to the dissenting chapels of the present day; for all that was required, and, indeed, what was most appropriate for the new form, was a large room well-aired, well-ventilated, a pulpit in such a situation that all the congregation might hear and see well, a communion-table in the middle[12], and two or three tiers of galleries, by means of which a large auditory might be crammed into a small space.

The old buildings are the very reverse of all this, and totally unfit for any worship but that for which they had been erected; but there they were, and, fitting or not, they were used for the new service, hence comes all the incongruities we see in all ancient parochial churches. The aisles cut to pieces by galleries of all sizes, and heights; the nave blocked up with pews; screens cut away; stalls removed from their old position in the chancel, and set about in odd places; chauntry chapels turned into corporation pews; wooden panelling, of execrable design, smeared over with paint, set up with the creed and commandments, entirely covering some fine tabernacle work, the projecting parts of which have been cut away to receive it. Large portions of the church, for which there is no use, walled off, to render the preaching place more snug and comfortable, porches enclosed and turned into engine houses, and a host of other wretched mutilations; and, when all has been done, what are they but inconvenient, inappropriate buildings, for the purpose they are used for? And, I am grieved to say, these enormities are not confined to obscure villages, or even large parochial churches: abominations equally vile with those I have above stated, and far more reprehensible, as proceeding from men whose name, education, and station, would have led us to hope for better things, are to be found in collegiate and cathedral churches, which are under the control of the highest class, as

---

[12] See Appendix, L.

in those edifices which are confided to the management of the brutal and the ignorant.

I have now, I trust, shewn how intimately the fall of architectural art in this country, is connected with the rise of the established religion.

I first shewed the stop it received under the destructions of the rapacious Henry, and consequent loss of those feelings, by which it had been carried on so successfully, for many centuries.

I then exhibited how avarice and fanaticism, both produced by the growth of the new opinions, had plundered and destroyed all those splendid efforts of art, which, under the fostering care of the ancient faith, enriched and embellished every sacred pile.

Further, I have shewn to what base and sordid motives we are indebted for the preservation of what is now left j and, lastly, I have shewn that, in order to render the churches at all available to the new system, they destroyed every grand feature about them, and rendered them both unsightly and inappropriate.

There is one more result which I have not yet described, but it is one of the most dreadful, the most disastrous, and one which effectually prevents the possibility of achieving great ecclesiastical works: it is the entire loss of religious unity among the people. When the Common Prayer and Articles had been set forth, heavy fines were imposed, and even death was inflicted, on all who did not receive them as the only rule of faith or form of religious worship[13]; and by such means as these, men had been driven for a short time into an outward show of uniformity. But where was the inward unity of soul-where that faith that had anciently bound men together? Alas! that was utterly fled. Where were the spontaneous offerings, the heartfelt tribute, the liberal endowments, by which the ancient church had been supported, and the glorious works achieved? The scene was entirely changed, and not only had these feelings ceased, but the commonest and most necessary repairs of those very buildings, which had been raised in splendour by the voluntary offerings of the people, were only effected by rates, wrung by fear of law from the unwilling parishioners, two-thirds of whom, from different motives, equally detested the form that had been forced upon them, and which they were compelled to support. No longer were village priests looked on as pastors of the people, or those high in ecclesiastical authority with veneration and respect; the former were considered only as a sort of collectors, placed to receive dues they were compelled to pay, while the latter were eyed with jealousy by the avaricious

---

[13] See Appendix, M.

nobles[14], and looked on by the majority of the people as a useless class of state officers. The increase of these feelings within one century of its first establishment caused the overthrow of the new religion, and the entire suspension of its functions, during the rule of the usurper, Cromwell, a period of English history too well known to need dilating on; and which same feelings attended its revival with the restoration of the Stuarts, and do at this present day, with threatening aspect, menace its utter downfal.

---

[14] See Appendix, N.

CHAPTER V
ON THE PRESENT DEGRADED STATE OF ECCLESIASTICAL BUILDINGS.

The spot that angels deigned to grace,
Is blessed though robbers haunt the place.

I will now proceed to examine the present state of ancient Ecclesiastical Buildings, after three centuries of mingled devastation, neglect, and vile repair have passed over them.

In the first place, I will commence with the cathedrals, the most splendid monuments of past days which remain, and, therefore, the most deserving of first consideration.

No person thoroughly acquainted with ecclesiastical antiquities, and who has travelled over this country for the purpose of attentively examining those wonderful edifices, which, though shorn of more than half their beauties, still proudly stand pre-eminent over all other structures that the puny hand of modem times has raised beside them, but must have felt the emotions of astonishment and admiration, that their first view has raised within him, rapidly give place to regret and disgust at the vast portion of them that has been wantonly defaced, and for the miserable unfitness of the present tenants for the vast and noble edifices they occupy.

When these gigantic churches were erected, each portion of them was destined for a particular use, to which their arrangement and decoration perfectly corresponded. Thus the choir was appropriated solely to the ecclesiastics, who each filled their respective stalls; the nave was calculated for the immense congregation of the people, who, without reference to rank or wealth, were promiscuously mixed in the public worship of God; while the aisles afforded ample space for the solemn processions of the clergy.

The various chapels, each with its altar, were served by different priests, who at successive hours of the morning, commencing at six, said masses, that all classes and occupations might be enabled to devote some portion of the day to religious duties. The cloisters formed a quiet and sheltered deambulatory for the meditation of the ecclesiastics; and the chapter-house was a noble chamber, where they frequently met and settled on spiritual and temporal affairs relating to their office.

These churches were closed only for a few hours. during the night, in order that they might form the place from whence private prayers and supplications might continually be offered up. But of what use are these churches now? do their doors stand ever open to admit the devout? No; excepting the brief space of time set apart twice a-day to keep up the form of worship, are the gates fast closed, nor is it possible to obtain admittance within the edifice without a fee to the guardian of the keys. Ask the reason of this, and the answer will be, that if the churches were left open they would be completely defaced, and even become the scene of the grossest pollutions. If this be true, which I fear it is, what, I ask, must be the moral and religious state of a country, where the churches are obliged to be fastened up to prevent their being desecrated and destroyed by the people? how must the ancient devotion and piety have departed? Indeed, 80 utterly are all feelings of private devotion lost in these churches, that were an individual to kneel in any other time than that actually set apart for Divine service, or in any other part of the edifice but that which is inclosed, he would be considered as a person not sound in his intellects, and probably be ordered out of the building. No; cathedrals are visited from far different motives by the different classes of persons who go to them. The first are those who, being connected with or living near a cathedral, attend regularly every Sunday by rote; the second are those who, not having any taste for prayers, but who have some ear for music, drop in, as it is termed, to hear the anthem; the third class are persons who go to see the church. They are tourists; they go to see every thing that is to be seen, therefore they see the church - *id est*, they walk round, read the epitaphs, think it very pretty, very romantic, very old, suppose it was built in superstitious times, pace the length of the nave, write their names on a pillar, and whisk out, as they have a great deal more to see and very little time.

The fourth class are those who, during assize and fair times, go to see the big church built by the old Romans, after they have been to see all the other sights and shows. They are generally a good many together, to make it worth the verger's while to send a satellite round with them to shew the wonderful things, and tell them wonderful stories about the monks and nuns; and after they have gaped round they go out, and the sight serves for talk till they see some fun they like a good deal better.

Such are most of the classes of visitors to these wondrous fabrics, not one of whom feel in the slightest degree the sanctity of the place or the majesty of the design, and small indeed is the number of those on whom these mutilated but still admirable designs produce their whole and great effect. Few are there who, amid the general change and destruction they have undergone, can con-. jure up in their minds the glories of their departed greatness, and who, while they bitterly despise the heartless throng that gaze about the sacred aisles, mourn for the remembrance of those ages of faith now passed and gone, which produced minds to conceive and zeal to execute such mighty, glorious works. 'Tis such minds as these that feel acutely the barren, meagre, and inappropriate use to which these edifices have been put; and to them does the neat and modern churchman appear truly despicable, as he trips from the door to the vestry, goes through the prayers, then returns from the vestry to the door, forming the greatest contrast of all with the noble works which surround him. What part has he, I say, what connexion of soul with the ecclesiastic of ancient days? Do we see him, when the public service is concluded, kneeling in silent devotion in the quiet retreat of some chapel? Do we see him perambulating in study and contemplation those vaulted cloisters, which were erected solely for the meditation of ecclesiastical persons? No; he only enters the church when his duty compels him; he quits it the instant he is able; he regards the fabric but as the source of his income; he lives by religion - 'tis his trade. And yet these men of cold and callous hearts, insensible to every spark of ancient zeal and devotion, will dare to speak with contempt and ridicule of those glorious spirits by whose mighty minds and liberal hearts those establishments have been founded, and from whose pious munificence they derive every shilling they possess.

Have they not common decent gratitude? No; daily do they put forth revilings, gross falsehoods, and libels, on that religion and faith which instigated the foundation and endowments which they enjoy, and under whose incitement alone could the fabrics have been raised which they pretend to admire, while they condemn and ridicule the cause which produced them.

Can we hope for any good results while such men as these use, or rather possess, these glorious piles 1 men who either leave the churches to perish through neglect, or when they conceive they have a little taste, and do layout some money, commit far greater havoc than even time itself by the unfitness and absurdity of their alterations. Of this description were those made by Bishop Barrington at Salisbury, and conducted by James Wyatt, of execrable memory, deserve the severest censure. During this improvement, as it was termed, the venerable bell-tower, a grand and imposing structure, which stood on the north-west side of the church, was demolished, and the bells and materials sold; the Hungerford and Beauchamp chapels pulled down, and the tombs set up in the most mutilated manner between the pillars of the nave, and a host of other barbarities and alterations too numerous to recite.

Nor less detestable was the removal of the ancient tracery and glass from the great eastern and aisle windows of St. George's Chapel, Windsor, and substituting copies of that tame and wooden painter, West-designs which would be a disgrace in any situation, and, when thus substituted for the masterly arrangement of the ancient architect, become even more detestable. In fine, wherever we go, we find that, whether the buildings have been treated with neglect, or attempted to be improved, both results are disastrous in the extreme.

The fact cannot for one moment be denied, that these edifices are totally unsuited for the purpose of the present establishment, quite deficient in what is now so much studied-comfort; and since the choir has been applied to the purpose of a parish church, totally wanting in actual sitting room, to gain which the ancient features are being rapidly swept away. What can be so disgusting as to enter the choir of a cathedral church, and find the stalls nominally appropriated to the dignitaries of the church, occupied by all classes of lay persons, and not unfrequently the bishop's throne, the cathedra itself, tenanted during the absence of the bishop by some consequential dame. Nay, so entirely is propriety of arrangement or decorum lost in these churches, that were it not for the presence of a few singing men and boys, and the head of a solitary residentiary peeping above his cushion, one would conclude the assembled group to be a congregation of independents, who had occupied the choir for a temporary preaching place; then the concluding rush out, when singing men, choristers, vicars, and people, make a simultaneous movement to gain the choir-door, produces a scene of the most disgraceful confusion. All this has arisen from the alteration of the ancient arrangement of appropriating the choir solely to ecclesiastics; but this was abandoned by the new churchmen on the consideration that they could never muster a decent show, and so they let the people in to hide the deficiency of their absence.

This led to pewing choirs, one of the vilest mutilations of effect the cathedrals have ever suffered; for what do all the alterations that have lately been effected in Peterborough and Norwich cathedrals tend, but utterly to destroy the appearance of a choir, filling up the centre with pews and seats, and contracting the grandeur of the open space into a paltry aisle leading to boxes.

It is in vain to cover the fronts of these seats with tracery and panelling; the principle of the thing is bad, and all that is done only renders the defect more glaring.

This picture of the modern state of cathedrals is forcible, but it is not over-drawn; anyone may be satisfied of its truth by inspecting the edifices themselves, and the manner in which the services are conducted.

Go to that wonderful church at Ely, and see the result of neglect: the water, pouring through unclosed apertures in the covering, conveying ruin into the heart of the fabric; the opening fissures. of the great western tower, which, unheeded and unobserved, are rapidly extending. Then look at what was once the Lady Chapel, but now filled with pews and vile fittings, brought from the parish church the chapter refused to repair[15]; see how the matchless canopies have been pared down and whitewashed. Look on the decay of the whole church, and then remember Ely is yet rich in its revenues. What must be the hearts of those men forming the chapter? And yet they are but a fair type of most of the others; I only cite them in particular, because Ely is one of the most interesting churches in existence, and it is decidedly in a vile state of repair.

The same observations will apply to most of the other great churches. Why, Westminster Abbey itself, by far the finest edifice in the metropolis, if cleared of its incongruous and detestable monuments, is in a lamentable state of neglect, and is continually being disfigured by the erection of more of vile masses of marble. Having occasion lately to examine the interior of this wonderful church, I was disgusted beyond measure at perceiving that the chapel of St, Paul had been half filled up with a huge figure of James Watt, sitting in an armchair on an enormous square pedestal, with some tasteless ornaments which, being totally unlike any Greek or Roman foliage, I suppose to have been intended by the sculptor to be Gothic. This is the production of no less a personage than Sir F. Chantrey. Surely this figure must have been originally intended for the centre of some great terrace-garden; it never could have been designed for the interior of the abbey: for so offensive is it in its present position, that if Sir Francis did really so design it, he deserves to be crushed under its great pedestal, to prevent him again committing so great an outrage on good taste.

But is this noble edifice for ever to be blocked up and mutilated by the continual erection of these most inappropriate and tasteless monuments? Are the fees so tempting to the dean, or has he no better feeling? But what can we expect or hope for from him or the chapter, when they suffer filthy

---

[15] See Appendix, O.

dolls to be exhibited within the sacred walls, to render the show-place more attractive to their shilling customers? Oh, spirits of the departed abbots, could you behold this! The mighty buildings you have raised, the tombs of the great men that lie within them - all is not attractive enough for the mob; a set of puppets are added, the show draws, and the chapter collects the cash. Oh, vile desecration! Yet this takes place in the largest church of the metropolis, the mausoleum of our kings; a place rendered of the highest interest by the art of its construction, and the historical recollections attached to it.

Can we, then, wonder at what I before asserted and, I trust, have since proved, that cathedral churches are become but show-places for the people, and considered only as sources of revenue by ecclesiastics?

I am willing, however, to allow that there has been a vast improvement of late years in the partial restorations which have been effected in certain cathedral and other churches, as regards the accuracy of moulding and detail. The mechanical part of Gothic architecture is pretty well understood, but it is the principles which influenced ancient compositions, and the soul which appears in all the former works, which is so lamentably deficient; nor, as I have before stated, can they be regained but by a restoration of the ancient feelings and sentiments. 'Tis they alone that can restore Gothic architecture to its former glorious state; without it all that is done will be a tame and heartless copy, true as far as the mechanism of the style goes, but utterly wanting in that sentiment and feeling that distinguishes ancient design.

It is for this reason that the modern alterations in the choirs of Peterborough and Norwich, above alluded to, have so bad an effect; the details individually are accurate and well worked, but the principle of the design is so contrary to the ancient arrangement, that I do not hesitate to say the effect is little short of detestable.

The same thing may be remarked at Canterbury, where I am happy to make honourable mention of the restorations. A great deal of money has been expended, and, I may add, judiciously; indeed the rebuilding of the north-western tower is an undertaking quite worthy of ancient and better days.

In these works, as far as recutting mouldings, pateras, bosses, &c., and the repainting and gilding, nothing can be better executed; but when we come to see the new altar-screen, as it is termed, we are astonished that amid so much art as this vast church contains, some better idea had not suggested itself. It is meagre and poor in the extreme, and not one particle of ancient sentiment about it - it is a bare succession of panels; but this is the result of modern feelings. When this church was used for the ancient worship, the high altar was the great point of attraction: it was for the sacrifice continually there offered the church itself was raised; neither gold, jewels, nor silver, were spared in its decoration; on it the ancient artists, burning with zeal and devotion, expended their most glorious compositions and skill. The mass was gorgeous and imposing; each detail, exquisite and appropriate. Such a design as this was not produced by multiplying a panel till it reached across the choir, nor was it composed to back a common table. No; the artist felt the glory of the work he was called on to compose; it was no less than erecting an altar for the performance of the most solemn rites of the church, and it was the glorious nature of the subject fined his mind with excellence, and produced the splendid result. From such feelings as these all the ancient compositions emanated; and I repeat that without them Gothic architecture can never rise beyond the bare copy of the mechanical portions of the art.

There is no sympathy between these vast edifices and the Protestant worship. So conscious of it were the first propagators of the new doctrines, that they aimed all their malice and invectives against them. The new religion may suit the conventicle and the meeting-house, but it has no part in the glories of ancient days; the Anglican church is the only one, among the many religions that sprung up, which retained the shadow of cathedral and episcopal establishments and so badly put together was this jumble of ancient church government with modern opinions and temporal jurisdiction, that it has ever proved the subject of popular clamour, and from present appearances we may judge it will ere long be entirely changed.

What a prospect to look to! What new ordeal, what new destruction are these ill-fated fabrics to undergo? The mind shudders at the thought. Are they to be walled up as in Scotland, and be divided into the preaching houses for the dissenters, the Unitarians, and the freethinkers? Are they to be made into factories and storehouses, like the churches of France during the fatal revolution of 1790? or are they, ruined and roofless, neglected, to decay like the many glorious fabrics that perished at the change of religion, of which only a few mouldering arches remain to indicate the site? One of these results must be produced whenever the present establishment ceases to exist. Let no one be deceived; such is the fate that awaits the cathedrals of this country. One ray of hope alone darts through the dismal prospect; it is that, ere the fatal hour arrives, so many may have returned into the bosom of the Catholic church, that hearts and hands may be found willing and able to protect these glorious piles from further profanation, and, in the real spirit of former years, restore them to their original glory and worship.

If we turn from the cathedrals themselves, to examine the ecclesiastical buildings with which they are surrounded, we shall find the changes and destructions they have undergone, to suit the caprice and ideas of each new occupant, are so great, that it is with considerable difficulty any thing like the original design can be traced.

All the ancient characteristic features have been totally changed, for after the clergy had left off ecclesiastical discipline for ease and comfort; exchanged old hospitality for formal visiting; and, indeed, become laymen in every other respect but that of their income and title. They found the old buildings but ill suited to their altered style of living; what had served for the studious, retired priest, or the hospitable and munificent prelate of ancient days, was very unfit for a married, visiting, gay clergyman, or a modern bishop, whose lady must conform to the usages and movements of fashionable life.

Hence bishops' palaces have either been pulled down, and rebuilt on a mean and reduced scale, or their grandest features left to decay as useless portions of the building, and the inhabited part repaired in the worst possible taste. Nor have the rectories and canonries escaped even worse treatment: many of the old buildings have been entirely demolished, and some ugly square mass set up instead; and all have been miserably mutilated: the private chapel every where demolished, or applied to some menial purpose;[16] the old oak. ceilings plastered up; the panelling removed, or papered over; mullioned windows cut out, and common sashes fixed in their stead; great plain brick buildings added to get some large rooms for parties; a veranda, and perhaps a conservatory. And by such means as these the canonries are rendered habitable for the three months' residence.

Then, if we examine the buildings that were anciently erected for the residence of the vicars attached to cathedrals, as at Wells, what a lamentable change have they undergone! When these buildings were constructed, the vicars were a venerable body of priests, living in a collegiate manner within their close; each one had a lodging or set of two chambers, a common hall where they assembled at meals, and a chapel, over which was a library stored with theological and classical learning, stood at opposite ends of the close. All these buildings were of the most beautiful description, and received great additions from the munificent Bishop Beckington; and so excellent is the arrangement of every part of this close, and its connexion with the cathedral by a corridor passing over a sumptuous gatehouse, and leading to the chapter-house stair, is so admirably managed, that, notwithstanding the vile repairs and mutilations it has suffered, and its present degraded condition, it is still one of the most interesting specimens of ecclesiastical buildings attached to cathedrals, and will give an excellent idea of the venerable character the residences of ecclesiastics formerly presented, and the unison of their appearance with that of the structures to

---

[16] See Appendix, P.

which they formed the appendages.

But no sooner was the blasting influence of the new religion felt, than this abode of piety and learning experienced a fatal change. The vicars were reduced to less than a third of their original number, and their lands so pillaged, that this ecclesiastical function was given to laymen, whose only qualification was a trifling skill in vocal music, that the poor pittance they had left, although quite insufficient for the support of persons devoted to the duties of their office, might still induce the needy shopkeeper to leave his counter twice in the day, hurry over the service, to return again to his half-served customers.

When the buildings, raised by the munificence of Roger de Salopia and Thomas de Beckington, fell into the hands of such men as these, the result may easily be imagined.

Gradually they sunk into neglect and decay; the dwellings rented to various tenants, who altered and changed them to their pleasure; the great hall used only when some newly arrived mountebank required a large room to exhibit his feats of dexterity, when it was let out for the occasion, or to serve the even meaner purpose of a dancing academy.

The library was of little use to such men as these, who never required any other book but that of their shop-accounts; and who, if they ever handled a classic author, it was only to convert the pages into wrappers for their parcels.

We cannot, therefore, feel surprised that a few odd leaves of manuscripts, and some imperfect and musty volumes of books, thrown into a corner of the muniment room, are all that remain of a collection, which the learning of its founders leaves us no hesitation in supposing to have been as useful as interesting and curious.

To such a degraded state are these lay vicars, as they are termed, fallen, that even the keeper of a public tavern is found among their number. Thus, this man, fresh from the fumes of the punch-bowl and tobacco-pipe, and with the boisterous calls of the tap ringing in his ears, may be seen running from the bar to the choir, there figuring away in a surplice, till the concluding prayer allows him to rush back, and mingle the response of "Coming, sir," to the amen that has hardly died away upon his lips.

How can we wonder at the contempt into which the establishment has fallen, when such disgraceful scenes as these have arisen from its system? Where, I ask, are the often boasted blessings which the misnamed Reformation has brought? where the splendid results so often asserted 1 Facts speak for themselves; and, I trust, I have brought forward a sufficient number to shew how dreadfully all classes of ecclesiastical buildings and persons have been ruined and degraded by the introduction of the present system.

If the limits of this work permitted, I could fully shew how baneful and disastrous to art were the effects produced by the Protestants in those foreign countries where they were, at one time, partially established; and even in France, where their ascendency only lasted the brief space of a year, they committed such havoc, that the principal treasures of the churches, and most of the finest specimens of art, were plundered and demolished; and ecclesiastical Architecture received a blow it has never since recovered, which the unfinished state of many of the finest edifices of Normandy, all discontinued at that period, amply testify[17].

Indeed, whether we regard the fanatic Knox in Scotland, the Huguenots of France, the compilers and concocters of the Anglican church, or the puritanic faction of Cromwell, we find that, divided as they were on points of their schismatical religions, they were united, heart and hand, in robbery and destruction[18]. To them sanctity or art were alike indifferent; thirst of gold and wanton love of destroying all which exceeded their narrow comprehensions, mingled with the most savage fanaticism, led them to commit crimes and disorders harrowing to the soul, both on the score of common humanity and the love of noble art[19].

That these feelings have partially subsided, is purely owing to the lukewarm feelings that religion is regarded by the majority in this country; since, only a few years back, the mere sight of a crucifix or a Madonna would have excited far greater horror, and caused more animadversion amongst the godly of the land, than the most obscene and filthy idol that the grossest superstition of paganism could produce[20]; and I do not hesitate to say, that there are many, among the fanatical sects which come under the general denomination of dissenters, who would exult in the destruction not only of every noble religious edifice that remains, but glory in the extinction of all ecclesiastical authority whatever.

I cannot conclude this part of my subject without making a few observations on the present system of church and chapel building-a system so vile, so mercenary, and so derogatory to the reverence and honour that should be paid to Divine worship, that it is deserving of the severest censure; and I will say, that among the most grievous sins of the time, may

---

[17] See Appendix, Q.

[18] See Appendix, R.

[19] See Appendix, S.

[20] See Appendix, T.

be ranked those of trying for how small a sum religious edifices can be erected, and how great a per centage can be made for money advanced for their erection by the rental of pews. It is a trafficking in sacred things, that vastly resembles that profanation of the temple which drew such indignation from our Divine Redeemer, that, contrary to the mild forbearance he had ever before shewn, he cast forth the polluters of the holy place with scourges and stripes.

Yes; the erection of churches, like all that was produced by zeal or art in ancient days, has dwindled down into a mere trade. No longer is the sanctity of the undertaking considered, or is the noblest composition of the architect, or the most curious skill of the artificer, to be employed in its erection; but the minimum it can be done for is calculated from allowing a trifling sum to the room occupied for each sitting; and the outline of the building, and each window, moulding, and ornament, must be made to correspond with this miserable pittance.

Of the feelings with which the old churchmen undertook the erection of their churches we can easily be acquainted, by referring to the solemn office of the dedication:

Domus quam ædificari volo Domino, talis esse debet, ut in cunctis regionibus nominetur; præparabo, ergo, ei necessaria.

Magnus est Deus noster super omnes deos; quis, ergo, poterit præbalere ut ædificet dignam Deo domum. Domine Deus noster, omnis hæc copia, quam parabimus ut ædificaretur domus nomini sancto tuo, de manu tua est. Quis prior Domino dedit, et retribuetur ei?

The church commissioners' instructions are the very reverse of these noble sentiments. They require a structure as plain as possible, which can be built for a trifling sum, and of small dimensions, both for economy and facilities of hearing the preacher, the sermon being the only part of the service considered; and I hesitate not to say, that a more meagre, miserable display of architectural skill never was made, nor more impropeties and absurdities committed[21]. than in the mass of paltry churches erected under the auspices of the commissioners, and which are to be found scattered over every modem portion of the metropolis and its neighbourhood - a disgrace to the age, both on the score of their composition, and the miserable sums that have been allotted for their construction.

No kind of propriety or fitness has been considered in their composition. Some have porticoes of Greek temples, surmounted by steeples of miserable outline and worse detail. Others are a mixture of distorted Greek and Roman buildings; and a host have been built in

---

[21] See Appendix, U.

perfectly nondescript styles, forming the most offensive masses of building. In some cases, the architect has endeavoured to give the shell the appearance of an ancient pointed church, and, by dint of disguising all the internal arrangements, something like an old exterior has been obtained; but when the interior is seen the whole illusion vanishes, and we discover that what had somewhat the appearance of an old Catholic church is, in reality, nothing but a modem preaching-house, with all its galleries, pews, and other fittings. In fine, so impossible is it to make a grand design suitable to the meagreness of the established worship, that to produce any effect at all, the churches are designed to represent any thing but what they really are; and hence, all the host of absurdities and incongruities, in form and decoration, which abound in modem places built for religious worship.

With respect to the style of that class of chapels built on speculation, it is below criticism. They are erected by men who ponder between a mortgage, a railroad, or a chapel, as the best investment of their money, and who, when they have resolved on relying on the persuasive eloquence of a cushion-thumping, popular preacher, erect four walls, with apertures for windows, cram the same full of seats, which they readily let; and so greedy after pelf are these chapel-raisers, that they form dry and spacious vaults underneath, which are soon occupied, at a good rent, by some wine and brandy merchant.

Of the horrible impiety of trading in religious edifices I have spoken more fully above, and, I repeat, that no offence can sooner move the indignation of the Almighty, or provoke his vengeance, than such a prostitution of the name of religion to serve the private interests of individuals.

In conclusion, although I would not, for one instant, deny that prayers, offered from the humblest edifice that can be raised, would prove as available and acceptable as if proceeding from the most sumptuous fabric, if the means of the people could produce no better. Yet, when luxury is every where on the increase, and means and money more plentiful than ever, to see the paltry buildings erected every where for religious worship, and the neglected state of the ancient churches, it argues a total want of religious zeal, and a tepidity towards the glory of Divine worship, as disgraceful to the nation, as it must be offensive to the Almighty.

CONCLUSION
ON THE WRETCHED STATE OF
ARCHITECTURE AT THE PRESENT DAY.

Perhaps there is no theme which is more largely dilated on, in the present day, than the immense superiority of this Century over every other that has preceded it. This great age of improvement and increased intellect, as it is called, is asserted to have produced results which have never been equalled; and, puffed up by their supposed excellence, the generation of this day look back with pity and contempt on all that passed away before them.
In some respects, I am willing to grans, great and important inventions have been brought to perfection: but, it must be remembered, that these are purely of a mechanical nature; and I do not hesitate to say, that as works of this description progressed, works of art and productions of mental vigour have declined in a far greater ratio.

Were I to dilate on this subject, I feel confident I could extend this principle throughout all the branches of what are termed the fine arts; but as my professed object is to treat on Architecture, I will confine my observations to that point, leaving to some more able hand the task of exposing false colour and superficial style, which has usurped nature of effect and severity of drawing, and of asserting the immense superiority of the etchings of the old schools over the dry and mechanical productions of the steel engravers of our time, whose miserable productions, devoid of soul, sentiment, or feeling, are annually printed by the thousand, and widely circulated, to remain an everlasting disgrace on the era in which they were manufactured.

Let us now, therefore, examine the pretensions of the present Century to a superiority in architectural skill; let us examine the results - that, is, the edifices that have been produced: and, I feel confident, we shall not be long in deciding that, so far from excelling past ages, the architectural works of our time are even below par in the scale of real excellence.

Let us look around, and see whether the Architecture of this country is not: entirely ruled by whim and caprice. Does locality, destination, or character of a building, form the basis of a design? no; surely not. We have Swiss cottages in a flat country; Italian villas in the coldest situations; a Turkish kremlin for a royal residence; Greek temples in crowded lanes; Egyptian auction rooms; and all kinds of absurdities and incongruities: and not only are separate edifices erected in these inappropriate and unsuitable styles, but we have only to look into those nests of monstrosities, the Regent's Park and Regent Street, where all kind of styles are jumbled together to make up a mass.

It is hardly possible to conceive that persons, who had made the art of Architecture the least part of their study, could have committed such enormities as are existing in every portion of these buildings. Yet this is termed a great metropolitan improvement: why, it is a national disgrace, a stigma on the taste of the country; and so it will remain till the plaster and cement, of which it is composed, decay.

Of an equally abominable description are the masses of brick and composition which have been erected in what are termed watering-places, particularly at Brighton, the favoured residence of royalty, and the sojourn of all the titled triflers who wait upon the motions of the court. In this place the vile taste of each villa and terrace is only surpassed by the royal palace itself, on which enormous sums have been lavished, amply sufficient to have produced a fabric worthy of a kingly residence. It would be an endless task to point out and describe all the miserable edifices that have been erected, within the last Century, in every class of Architecture; suffice it to observe, that it would be extremely difficult, if not impossible, to find one amongst the immense mass which could be handed down to succeeding ages as an honourable specimen of the architectural talent of the time.

This is a serious consideration, for it is true. Where, I ask, are the really fine monuments of the country to be found, but in those edifices erected centuries ago, during the often railed at and despised period of the Middle Ages! What would be the interest of the cities, or even towns and villages, of this country, were they deprived of their ancient gigantic structures, and the remains of their venerable buildings 1 Why, even in the metropolis itself, the abbey church and hall of Westminster still stand pre-eminent over every other ecclesiastical or regal structure that has since been raised.

No one can look on Buckingham Palace, the National Gallery, Board of Trade, the new buildings at the British Museum, or any of the principal buildings lately erected, but must feel the very existence of such public monuments as a national disgrace.

And if we regard the new castle at Windsor, although the gilding and the show may dazzle the vulgar and the ignorant, the man of refined taste and knowledge must be disgusted with the paucity of ideas and meagre taste which are shewn in the decoration; and he will presently discover, that the elongated or extended quatrefoil and never-ending set of six pateras, in the rooms called Gothic, and the vile scroll-work intended for the :flowing style of Louis Quatorze, announce it as being the work of the plasterer and the putty presser, instead of the sculptor and the artist.

Nor is there to be found among the residences of the nobility, either in their town mansions or country seats, lately erected, any of those imposing and characteristic features, or rich and sumptuous ornaments, with which the residences of the Tudor period abounded.

Nor can any thing be more contemptible than the frittered appearance of the saloons and galleries, crowded with all sorts of paltry objects, arranged, as if for sale, in every corner, which have replaced the massive silver ornaments, splendid hangings, and furniture of the olden time.

Indeed, I fear that the present general feeling for ancient styles is but the : result of the fashion of the day, instead of being based on the solid foundation I of real love and feeling for art itself; for, I feel confident, if this were not the Lease, purchasers could never be found for the host of rubbish annually imported and sold: nor could persons, really acquainted with the beauty of what they profess to admire, mutilate fine things when they possess them, by altering their greatest beauties to suit their own caprice and purposes-a barbarity continually practised in what is called. fitting-up old carvings.

Yes, believe me, this gout for antiquities is of too sudden a nature to have proceeded from any real conviction of the beauty of those two styles, or to have been produced from other motives but those of whim and fashion; and I do believe that, were some leading member of the *haut ton* to set the fashion for .some new style, the herd of collectors would run as madly after their new plaything, as they do after the one they have got at present.

The continual purchase of these things, at extravagant prices, may benefit the broker and the salesman, but does not advance a restoration of such art or style one iota.

Were these people of power and wealth really impressed with a feeling of admiration for the glorious works of ancient days, and anxious for the restoration of the skill and art which produced them, instead of filling their apartments with the stock of a broker's shop, they would establish a museum, where the finest specimens of each style might be found, and from which the sculptor and the artist might school themselves in their principles. They would send forth men to preserve faithful representations of the most interesting monuments of foreign lands, and extend a fostering care for the preservation and repair of those fine remains rapidly falling into decay; and, by encouraging talent where it is to be found, raise up by such means a race of artists, who, I hesitate not to say, could be found able to conceive and execute things equally fine and masterly as in more ancient days, but who, for want of such support, are compelled to leave the study of what they most admire, and in which they would excel, for some grovelling occupation by which to gain a bare subsistence.

I state this to wrest from these mere buyers of curiosities the title of patrons of art, which has so undeservedly been bestowed upon them. It was under! the fostering care of the Catholic church, and its noble encouragement, the I greatest efforts of art have been achieved; deprived of that, the arts in vain look, for an equivalent: for its professors must either starve neglected, or sacrifice the noblest principles and beauties of their art to the caprice and ignorance of their employers.

I could not refrain from making this digression, as I feel that what I have just stated is one of the great causes of the present wretched state of art.

I trust I have now shewn satisfactorily that this country, however it may excel in mechanical contrivances, has so little to boast on the score of improvement in art, that, were it not for the remains of the edifices produced during the Middle Ages, the architectural monuments of this country would be contemptible in the extreme.

The truth of this assertion, coupled with the fact that there never was a period when there were so many lectures, academies, drawing schools, and publications on the subject, proves how little the noble arts of Architecture, Painting, and Sculpture, are suited to the trammels of a system; and nothing has tended more to produce the vile results we see, than the absurd idea that persons can be brought up as easily to practise in those exalted professions, as to fill the humble station of a trafficker in merchandise or a mechanical trade; when, in truth, few are there who ever have, or ever can, attain to great excellence in the arts, and the station they arrive at must depend entirely on their own souls and exertions-for small indeed is the instruction that can be imparted on the subject, beyond the mere mechanical use of the tools, and the general principles of drawing.

It is quite lamentable to behold the manner in which good commonplace tradesmen by the present system are spoiled, and made into idle, unemployed, nominal architects, who either lounge about exhibition rooms, form societies, and pass the most sweeping censures on the finest productions of antiquity, because they have not sense enough to see their beauties; or, if through the interest of their friends they gain something to do, make frightful caricatures of Greek and Roman temples, which they designate as classic taste, or even viler compositions in the pointed style, where all proportion and propriety is so outraged; that the most beautiful features of the old buildings become disgusting and offensive when thus distorted and misapplied.

The cause which led these men to be educated, as it is called, for the profession, was most probably nothing more originally than scribbling on a slate; this was interpreted to signify a precocious talent for design, and after a few quarters under the school drawing-master, the youth is placed with some architect in town, who has acquired a name, and who will allow him to waste a few years in daily attendance at his office, for the consideration of some hundreds he receives with him. Here, at the appointed hours, he lolls over his desk, draws the five orders, then pricks off plans, and, when his apprenticeship is nearly expired, he may, perhaps, be able to rule the lines of an elevation clearly, and do a tolerably neat plan.

We next behold him admitted student at the Royal Academy, on the strength of having drawn out a portico, with a wing on each side, termed an original design, and shaded up the representation of two casts, bought at the nearest plaster shop. Here he idles a little more time, copies a few more casts, makes another composition; and perhaps be gets a medal, perhaps not. At any rate, it is time he set forth on His travels to classic shores; and thither, at a vast expense, is he sent, and three or four more years of the most precious period of life is spent in going over, for the thousandth time, the same set of measurements 011 the same set of cornices and columns. Here he obtains a smattering, and a vocabulary of names; and returns a conceited, bustling pretender. Three alternatives then offer; for either he gets business, makes vile designs, and, by the help of some practical man, builds them; or he remains a burden on his friends, and a mere coverer of exhibition walls with wretched compositions; or, if neither of these, he settles down into a common surveyor-a man who writes architect on his door and on his card, but who is, in reality, a measurer of land, a valuer of dilapidations, and a cutter-down of tradesmen's accounts.

Such are the results which are produced by the present system of architectural education; nor can great results ever be produced by such means. Architecture, that grandest of sciences, is fallen to a mere trade, and conducted not by artists, but by mere men of business.

All the mechanical contrivances and inventions of the day, such as plastering, composition, papier-maché, and a host of other deceptions, only serve to degrade design, by abolishing the variety of ornament and ideas, as well as the boldness of execution, so admirable and beautiful in ancient carved works.

What can be so ludicrous as to see one of these putty-stamping manufacturers, with a whole host of pieces, cutting, paring, brading on, and contriving an ornament 1 then covering over the whole with priming to hide the joints: and when done, it is a heavy, disjointed, ugly composition. Yet it is cheap-that is, it is cheaper than what an artist can design and produce; and, without regard to its wretched inferiority, it is stuck up - where? In the royal palaces, and in the mansions of the nobles. And this introduction of pressed putty ornaments, which the commonest labourers can squeeze, is called a distinguishing mark of increasing taste, and encouragement for, what is falsely termed, splendid decoration, but which is, in reality, only a love of cheap, gaudy, and vulgar show.

The just sense of all these various degradations, into which Architecture has fallen, together with the desire of representing the effect the pretended Reformation had on the Architecture of this country, induced me to undertake the publication of this volume.

I own the attempt is a bold one. Books have generally been written, and plates published, to suit private and party views and interests, in consequence of which the truth has generally been wofully disguised, and flattery and falsehood replaced sincerity and reality.

In this work I have been actuated by no other feelings but that of advancing the cause of truth over that of error.

I feel acutely the fallen condition of the arts, when each new invention, each new proceeding, seems only to plunge them deeper in degradation. I wish to pluck from the age the mask of superior attainments so falsely assumed, and I' am anxious to direct the attention of all back to the real merit of past and better days. It is among their remains that excellence is only to be found; and it is by studying the zeal, talents, and feelings, of these wonderful but despised times, that art can be restored, or excellence regained. (Laus Deo.)

A. WELBY PUGIN.

Contrasts

APPENDIX

A.

They (the visitors) represented their offences in such multiplying glasses, as made them seem both greater in number, and more horrid in nature, than indeed they were. – HEYLIN, p.262.

The commissioners threatened the canons of Leicester that they would charge them with adultery and unnatural crimes, unless they would consent to give up their house. – *See Hist. Collect.*, from 36 to 52.

Burnet owns that there were great complaints made of the violences and briberies of the visitors, and perhaps, says he, not without reason.- *Abrid.* p. 182.

The infamous Dr. London was appointed visitor to Godstowe Nunnery, of whose vile practices there the abbess, Catherine Bukley, complains most feelingly, in a letter addressed to the king, which may be seen at length in Steven's Continuation to Dugdale, p. 537. This same Dr. London was so abominable a character, that he was afterwards convicted of perjury, and adjudged to ride with his face to the horse's tail at Windsor and Oakingham, with papers about his head. – STEVEN'S *Continuation to Monasticon Anglicanum*, p. 538.

The learned and pious Abbot Whiting, of Glastonbury, was condemned in consequence of a book against the king's divorce, which had been introduced without his knowledge, being found in the abbey. This book was brought in solely for the purpose of accomplishing the ruin of this abbot, who firmly opposed the surrender of his abbey.

B.

In the month of November, Hugh Harringdon, Abbot of Reading, and two priests, named Rug and Orion, were hanged and quartered at

Reading. The same day was Richard Whiting, Abbot of Glastonbury, hanged and quartered on the Torre Hill beside his monastery. John Thome and Roger James, monks, the one treasurer, the other under-treasurer, of Glastonbury church, were at the same time executed; and, shortly after, John Beech, Abbot of Colchester, was executed at Colchester-all for denying the king's supremacy. – STOW'S *Chronicle*, p. 576.

The 29th of April, John, prior of the charter-house at London; Augustine Webster, Prior of Beuall; Thomas Laurence, Prior of Escham; Richard Reginalds, doctor, a monk of Sion; and John Hale, Vicar of Thistleworth; were all condemned of treason, for the supremacy, and were drawn, hanged, and quartered at Tyburn, the 4th day of May, 1538, their heads and quarters set on the gates of the city, all save one quarter, which was set on the charter-house, London. - STOW.

The 18th of June, three monks of the charter-house at London, named Thomas Exmew, Humfrey Middlemore, and Sebastian Nidigate, were drawn to Tyburn, and there hanged and quartered for denying the king's supremacy. - *Ibid.*

The 22d of June, Doctor John Fisher, Bishop of Rochester, for denying the king's supremacy, was beheaded on the Tower Hill; his head was set on London bridge, and his body buried within Barking church-yard. - *Ibid.*

The 6th of July, Sir Thomas More was beheaded on the Tower Hill for the like denial of the king's supremacy; and then the body of Doctor Fisher, Bishop of Rochester, was taken up, and buried with Sir Thomas More, both in the Tower.

The 10th of April, Sir William Peterson, priest, late Commissary of Calais; and Sir William Richardson, priest of St. Marie's, in Calais, were both there hanged, drawn, and quartered, in the market-place, for the supremacy. - *Ibid.*

These are only a few of the many persons this monster of cruelty executed for denying his supremacy. Indeed, it was the means he ridded himself of all churchmen, whose firmness and constancy were a barrier to his innovations.

C.

Within this clochier of St. Paul's were four very great bells, called Jesus Bells, in regard they specially belonged to Jesus Chapel, situate at the east end of the undercroft of St. Paul's; as also, on the top of the spire, the image of St. Paul: all standing, till Sir Miles Partridge, knight, *temp.* Henry VIII., having won them of the king *at one cast of the dice*, pulled them down. Which Sir Miles afterwards, *temp.* Edward VI., suffered death on Tower Hill, for matters relating to the Duke of Somerset. – DUGDALE'S *St.*

Paul's Cathedral, p. 128.

D.

Goodwin, speaking of a chapel which Stillington, Bishop of Wells, had built, adjoining the east side of the cloister there, and in which he was buried, says: -

"His body rested but a short time; for it is reported that diverse olde men, who in their youth had not only seene the celebration of his funeral, but also the building of, his tombe, chapell and all, did also see toombe and chapell destroyed, and the bones of the bishop that built them turned out of the lead in which they were interred. This chapel was destoyed by Sir John Gates, in the time of Edward VI.

E.

The following are among the executions on the score of religion in Henry's reign: -

Twenty-second of July, 1534, John Frith, for denying the real presence in the sacrament, the first executed in England for this cause. November, 1538, was John Lambert burnt in Smithfield for the same opinion.

And Stow mentioned sixteen different persons burnt for heresy; that is, holding, the present Protestant opinions. Fuller, Heylin, and other historians, shew that Cranmer sat in judgment, and signed the condemnation of many of these, for the very opinions he held himself privately.

F.

In 1540, the king summoned a parliament, to be holden at Westminster the 28th of April; also a synod of prelates, in which six articles were concluded, touching matters of religion, commonly called the whip with six strings.

Article 1 confirmed the real presence in the sacrament.

Article 2, against communion in both kinds.

Article 3, that priests might not marry after the order of priesthood received.

Article 4, that vows of chastity, made after twenty-one years of age, should be binding.

Article 5, the establishing of private masses.

Article 6, auricular confession to be expedient.

The punishment for the breach of the first article was burning without any abjuration, with loss of all goods and lands, as in case of treason; the default against the other five articles was felony, without benefit of clergy. - FOX'S *Martyrs*, edit. 1589.

It will be seen from these articles what little differences of doctrine caused Henry's separation from the Catholic church, and proves that he was moved to that step from temporal motives only.

It is, also, worthy of remark, that the leading apostle of the Reformation, Archbishop Cranmer, subscribed to these articles, and proceeded on them by condemning others, when, in fact, he secretly violated every one of them himself.

G.

In order to shew how soon the promiscuous use of the Holy Scriptures was found to produce baneful results, I have transcribed a portion of Henry's speech to his parliament, made in 1545, which gives a true and lively picture of the state of religious discord that had already risen, and the rapid demoralisation that attended the departure from the ancient system: -

"I see here daily you of the cleargie preach one against another, teach one contrary to another, inveigh one against the other, without charity or discretion; thus all men be in variety and discord, and few or none preacheth truly and sincerely the word of God. Alas! how can poor souls live in concord, when you preachers sow amongst them in your sermons debate and discord 1 if to you they look for light, and you bring them to darkness?

"Although I say the spiritual men be in fault, yet you of the temporality be not clear and unspotted of malice and envy, for you rail on bishops, speak slanderously of priests, and rebuke and taunt preachers; and, although you be permitted to read Holy Scriptures, and to have the word of God in your mother tongue, you most understand it is licensed you so to do only to inform your own consciences, and to instruct your children and families, and not to dispute and make a railing and taunting stock of Scripture against priests and preachers, as many light persons do. I am very sorry to know and hear how irreverently that most precious jewel, the word of God, is *disputed, ruined, sung, and tangled, in every alehouse and tavern*, contrary to the true meaning of the same. I am even as much sorry that the readers of the same follow it, in doing, so faintly and coldly; for of this I am sure, *charity was never so faint among you, vertuous and godly living was never less used, nor God himself amongst Christians never less reverenced, honored, or served.*" - HOLINSHED'S *Chronicle*, vol. ii. p. 972.

H.

Poynet, first Protestant bishop of Winchester, passed away all the temporalities of his see conditionally to his preferment to it, in return for which he was to receive certain rectories. – STRYPE, *Mem. Ecc.* vol. iii. p.

272.
Ridley, within nine days after his promotion to the see of London, alienated four of its best manors to the king, to gratify some of the courtiers. - *Ibid.* p. 234.

Barlow, at Wells, 20th May, 1548, consigned by license to the king a very considerable portion of the demesnes and manors of his see. - COLLINSON.

I.

The following are notes relative to these barbarous demolitions: -
Neither the Bishops of Lichfield and Coventry nor Llandaff had any recompense for their demolished palaces, according to Spelman; but Hooper, who had been chaplain to the Protector, had a house granted him in Whitefriars.

In the year 1549, on the 10th of April, the chapel in Pardon churchyard, by commandment of the Duke of Somerset, was begun to be pulled down, with the whole cloystrie, the dance of death, the tombs and monuments, so that nothing was left but the bare plot of ground, which has since been converted into a garden for petty canons – STOW'S *Survey*, p. 354.

In this chapel (standing on the north side of the churchyard) were buried Henry Barton, lord mayor of London, A.D. 1417, and Thomas Mirfin, mayor also in 1419, who had fair tombs therein, with their images in alabaster, strongly coped with iron; all which, with the chapel, were pulled down in anno 1549 (3 Edward VI.), by the Duke of Somerset's appointment, and made use of for his building at Somerset House in the Strand: the bones, which lay in the vault underneath, amounting to more than a thousand cart-loads, being conveyed into Finnesbury Fields, and there laid on a moorish place, with so much soil to cover them as did raise the ground for three windmills to stand on, which have since been built there. – DUGDALE'S *Hist. St. Pauls*, p. 130.

J.

In this month of April, and in May, commissioners were directed through England for all the church goods remaining in cathedral and parish churches-that is to say, jewels of gold and silver, silver crosses, candlesticks, censors, chalices, and such like, with their ready money, to be delivered to the master of the king's jewels in the Tower of London; all coapes and vestments of cloth of gold, cloth of tissue, and silver, to the master of the king's wardrobe in London; the other coapes, vestments, and ornaments, to be sold, and the money to be delivered to Sir Edward Peckham, knight: reserving church one chalice or cup, with table cloathes for the communion board, at the discretion of the commissioners, which were, for London, the lord mayor, the bishop, the lord chief justice, and other .- STOW'S *Chronicle*, p. 609.

K.

Harrington thus relates the ravages and spoliations at Wells: - Scarce were five years past after Bath's ruins, but as fast went the axes and hammers to work at Wells. The goodly hall, covered with lead (because the roofe might seeme too low for so large a roome), was uncovered; and now this roofe reaches to the sky. The chapell of our lady, late repaired by Stillington, a place of great reverence and antiquitie, was likewise defaced; and such was their thirst after lead (I would they had drunk it scalding), that they took the *dead bodies of bishops out of their leaden coffins, and cast abroad the carcases scarce thoroughly putrified.* The statues of brass, and all the antient monuments of kings, benefactors to that goodly cathedral church, went all the same way, sold to an alderman of London.

Furthermore, says Stow (speaking of St. Leonard's, Shoreditch), one vicar there (of late time), for covetousnesse of the brasse, which hee converted into coyned silver, plucked up many plates fixed on the graves, and left no memory of such as had been buried under them - a great injury both to the living and the dead, forbidden by public proclamation in the reigne of our soveraigne lady Queen Elizabeth, but not forborne by many, that, either of a preposterous zeale, or of a greedie minde, spare not to satisfie themselves by so wicked a meanes. – STOW'S *Survey*, p. 475.

L.

In order to do away, as much as possible, with the idea of an altar, the communion tables were placed away from the walls ; and when the high church party, under Charles I., attempted to place them again altarwise, as they are set at present, the zeal and opposition of the low church party gave rise to many disgraceful scenes and foolish pamphlets. A book, called "The Holy Table, Name, and Thing," tells us that, when the vicar of Grantham fell upon removing the communion table from the upper part of the choir to the altarplace, as he called it, Mr. Wheatly, the alderman, questioning him thereupon, what authority he had from the bishop, received this answer: that his authority was this-he had done it, and he would justify it. Mr. Wheatly commanded his officers to remove the place again, which they did accordingly, but not without STRIKING, much heat, and indiscretion, both of the one side and the other. The vicar said, he cared not what they did with their old tressel, for he would make him an altar of stone at his own charge, and :fix it in the old altar place, and would never officiate at any other; the people replying, that he should set up no dresser of stone in their church.

A letter was addressed to the vicar of Grantham about setting his table altarwise.

In answer to the letter comes out a book, entitled "A Coal from the Altar," which was answered again by the "Quench Coal." And this knotty point, where the table should stand, engaged a host of writers of the time.

M.

There is no period of English history which has been more disguised than the reign of that female demon, Elizabeth; for while her unfortunate sister has been stigmatised as bloody Mary, and ever held up to odium as an intolerant, persecuting bigot, Elizabeth has been loaded with encomiums, of which she is quite undeserving. The fact is, the church of England, while she had the power to be so, was the most intolerant that ever existed; and Elizabeth's reign exhibits a most frightful picture of savage persecution, carried on equally against those who professed the ancient religion, or those who carried Protestant principles further than the new churchmen thought advisable for the safety of their establishment.

During twenty years of her reign, two hundred and four persons were executed solely on the score of the Catholic religion. Of this number, one hundred and forty-two were priests; three, gentlewomen; and the remainder, esquires, gentlemen, and yeomen. Amongst these, fifteen were condemned for denying the queen's spiritual supremacy; one hundred and twenty-six, for the exercise of the priestly functions and the rest, for being reconciled to the Catholic faith, or for aiding and abetting priests.

Besides ninety priests, or Catholic lay persons, who died in prison, and one hundred and five who were sent into perpetual banishment; to say nothing of many more who were whipped, fined (the fine for recusancy was 20l. per month), or stripped of their property, to the utter ruin of their families.

In one night, fifty Catholic gentlemen, in the county of Lancaster, were suddenly seized and committed to prison, on account of their non-attendance at church. At the same time, an equal number of Yorkshire gentlemen were lying prisoners in York castle, on the same account, most of whom perished there. These were every week dragged by main force to hear the established service performed in the castle chapel. - DR. MILNER'S *Letters to a Prebendary.*

The torturing then in practice, Camden, in his annals, confirms; who, speaking of the famous Father Campian, says, he was not so racked but that he was still able to write his name.

It appears from the account of one of these sufferers, that the following tortures were in use against the Catholics in the Tower: - 1. The common rack, by which the limbs were stretched by levers; 2. The scavenger's daughter, so called, being a hoop in which the body was bent till the head and feet met together; 3. The chamber little-ease, being a hole so small, that a person could neither stand, sit, nor lie straight in it; 4. The iron gauntlet. - *Diar. Rar. Gest. in Turr. Lond.*

With what cruelty Catholics were racked, we may gather from the following passage in a letter from John Nicols to Cardinal Allen, by way of extenuating the guilt of his apostasy and perfidy in accusing his Catholic brethren: - Non bona res est corpus, isto cruciatu, longius fieri per duos ferè pedes quam natura concessit.

The continual harassing the Catholics suffered is amply shewn by the following extract: -

The 4th of April, being Palm Sunday, there was taken, saying of masse in the Lord Morleie's house, within Aldgate of London, one Albon Dolman, priest; and the Lady Morley, with her children, and divers others, were also taken for hearing the said masse. There was also taken, the same day and houer, for saying masse at the Lady Gilford's, in Trinitie Lane, one Oliver Heywood, priest; and, for hearing the said masse, the Lady Gilford, with diverse other gentlewomen. There was also taken, at the same instant, in the Lady Browne's house, in Cow Lane, for saying masse, one Thomas Heiwood, priest, and one John Couper, priest, with the Lady Browne; and diverse others were likewise taken for hearing of the said masse. All which persons were for the said offences indicted, convicted, and had the law according to the statute in that ease provided. There were also found in their several chappels diverse Latine books, beades, images, palms, chalices, crosses, vestments, pixes, paxes, and such like. –STOW'S *Chronicle*, p. 1158.

Death by burning, on the score of religion, was likewise practised: -
The 22d July, 1576, two Dutchmen, anabaptists, were burnt in Smithfield, who died in great horror with roaring and crying. – STOW'S *Chronicle*, p. 1162.

Mathew Hamont, of Hetharset, by his trade a ploughwright, three miles from Norwich, was convened before the Bishop of Norwich, for that he denied Christ to be our Saviour, and other heresies.

For which he was condemned in the consistory, and sentence was read against him by the Bishop of Norwich, the 14th of April, 1578, and thereupon delivered to the sherif18 of Norwich; and because he spake words of blasphemie against the queen's majesty, and others of her counsell, he was, by the recorder, Master Sergeant Wyndham, and the maior, Sir Robert Wood, condemned to lose both his eares, which were cut off, the 13th of May, in the market-place of Norwich; and afterwards, the 20th of Maie, he was burnt in the castle-ditch – STOW'S *Chronicle*, p. 1174.

Many more instances could be cited; but, I trust, sufficient has been shewn to prove that the system on which the church of England was founded and carried on, was the very acme of religious intolerance and persecution; and it is only very lately that Catholics have been relieved from degrading restrictions, which they continued to suffer after the more violent persecutions had ceased.

N.

The Earl of Leicester (favourite of Elizabeth) was at the head of those who said that no bishops ought to be tolerated in a Christian land, and that he had cast a covetous eye on Lambeth Palace. – HEYLIN'S *Hist. of Eliz.* p. 168.

O.

The magnificent lady chapel of Ely is now used as Trinity church, in consequence of the chapter assigning it to the parishioners, to save the expense of repairing the parish church, which they were bound to do; and the lamentable havoc that has been made in this once beautiful structure by the modem pewing, communion-screen, &c., and the fixing of some wretched monumental tablets, must be seen to be properly conceived. Owing to the same cause, three other cathedrals have been mutilated in a similar manner.

At Norwich cathedral, the ancient chapel of St. Luke, and the south aisle of the choir and apsis, have been inclosed and blocked up with pews, to serve as a parish church for St. Ethelbert's.

At Hereford, the north transept is inclosed and filled with pews, &c., to serve as a parochial church for the parishioners of St. John the Baptist.

At Chester, the south transept has been walled off, and serves for the parish church of St. Oswald's.

P.

Formerly not only the residences of ecclesiastics, but the houses of the laity were all provided with a private chapel, suitable to the size of the dwelling; but, alas! how is this feeling now changed? In vain do we look, in modern mansions, for a chamber devoted to religious worship; and in those ancient dwellings, where the piety of our ancestors had erected chapels, in how few instances do we find them still employed for their primitive destination? how often do we find they have been levelled to the ground as useless portions of the building? or, if not so, desecrated to the meanest purposes[22]? Rarely, among the canonries or ecclesiastical residences

---

[22] The ancient chapel of the Bishop of Ely's palace, at Ely, was used as a beer-cellar in 1834.

attached to cathedrals, can we find one that has been retained to its original use; and how can we imagine religion to dwell with those, who will not devote one small niche of their dwellings to her?

Domestic chapels and chaplains are alike falling into absolute disuse; they will soon be spoken of as things that used to be-as the remains of old superstition, and the relics of popery-the excuse made, whenever the establishment thinks proper to abolish any of the ancient practices and regulations which her founders had retained.

Q.

The excesses committed by the Huguenots and Calvinists in France, during the year 1562, are of so horrible and extensive a nature, that to give any thing like a narration of them would exceed the compass of a volume; but I have here subjoined a few notes, to prove to those who may be unacquainted with the subject, the truth of my assertion.

During the above-mentioned period, the whole of the rich ornaments belonging to the cathedral of Rouen were pillaged and melted, of which the high altar alone contained six hundred and eighty-two marks of silver, besides jewels and twenty-seven marks of pure gold, all wrought into the most beautiful forms. Not only did these sacrilegious wretches plunder all that was valuable, but with fanatic fury they consumed all the holy relics contained in the shrines, and treated the remains of St. Romain with the most barbarous indignity.

The cathedral was filled with stores of ammunition, and the Divine service totally suspended. DOM. POM. *Hist. Cath. Rouen.*

At the same time the magnificent abbey of St. Ouen, in the same city, was ravaged completely; not only were all the precious ornaments and vestments completely pillaged, but the fury of these miserable heretics was vented on the finest efforts of art the church contained. The rood-loft, unrivalled as a specimen of elaborate and wonderful masonry, was totally demolished; the stalls, burnt; all the brass work of the choir, which was of the finest description, torn down and melted j and even the tomb of the learned and munificent Abbe Marc D'Argent (founder and designer of this glorious church) fell a prey to their savage fury, and was totally destroyed.- *Histoire de l'Eglise de Saint Ouen, par* M. GILBERT. Paris, 1822.

July the 1st, a large party of Calvinists quitted Rouen for a predatory excursion, and, having burnt and pillaged several churches in the vicinity of Barentin, they re-entered Rouen in a sort of tumultuous triumph, some wearing chasubles, others copes, bearing the crosses in mockery, and tossing the chalices and thuribles in their hands by way of derision; some crying "Death of the mass," others, "Here is a death-blow to the Papists," and similar outrageous expressions. - DOM. POMERAYE *Hist. Cath.*

Rouen. Rouen, 1686, p. 126.

A manuscript chronicle of the Abbey of Jumièges relates, that two of the monks, going to Evereux to meet their abbot, Gabriel le Veneur, fell into the hands of a similar party; when they twisted whipcord round their foreheads so tightly, to make them reveal the place where the treasures of their abbey were concealed, that, their eyes starting from their sockets, one died from excess of agony immediately, and the other, Father Caumont, remained a miserable object till his death. - DOM. POM. *Hist. Cath. Rouen*, p. 162.

The 10th of May, 1562, being Sunday, the Protestants of Bayeux and its vicinity entered the cathedral church armed; and having instantly caused the cessation of high mass, then celebrating, they broke down the altars and images, and commenced pillaging the sacred vessels and ornaments. Those Catholic citizens and ecclesiastics who endeavoured to repress this outrage were immediately sacrificed, being either pistolled on the spot, or dragged to the walls, from which, after having their throats cut, they were immediately precipitated. The bishop, Charles de Humieres, and Germain Duval, the dean, only escaped the massacre by gaining the haven, from whence they put to sea in a small fishing-boat that happened to be lying there. - BEZIER'S *Histoire de la Ville de Bayeux*, p. 24.

The *verbal procès*, presented to the king by the bishop and clergy of Bayeux on the re-establishment of the ecclesiastics in 1563, gives a detailed account of all the destructions and robberies committed on the cathedral, while in possession of these fanatics. It is too long for insertion here, but the following facts may be gathered from it : - That every precious ornament whatever, as well as vestments of all descriptions, had been pillaged and destroyed; that a great portion of the stained windows were dashed out. The stalls, bishop's throne, chapel-screens, organ-case, and every description of wood carving, had been broken up and carried away. The charters, all archives belonging to the cathedral, had been burned, as well as the library. That the bodies of the ancient ecclesiastics, including the Patriarch de Harcour, had been disinterred, the bodies left exposed, and their coffins melted down. That all the brass work, consisting of effigies on tombs, an immense crown of admirable workmanship that hung in the choir, and other curious ornaments, had likewise been melted. That all the scaffolding, cords, pulleys, and materials, that were employed about the repair of the edifice, had been sold and removed. The ten great bells had been broken and melted, as well as the organ-pipes, and four thousand weight of lead from the roof, which had been cast into ammunition. Besides a great variety of other demolitions and acts of cruelty, practised on the ecclesiastics in the city, the whole of which are given at length in BEZIER'S *Histoire de la Ville de Bayeux*, beginning at page 3 of the

Appendix.

From these historical accounts of only a few of the very extensive outrages committed by the Protestants in France, I leave the candid and impartial reader to judge if I have gone too far in my assertion.

R.

To prove the truth of the great similarity of the various classes of Protestants in their outrages, I wish to refer the reader to the description of the demolitions at Wells, described in this Appendix under the letter K. I have also subjoined some extracts from an account of the excesses committed by the Puritans, during the civil wars, at Peterborough cathedral. Espying that rare work of stone over the altar, admired by all travellers, they made all of it rubbish, breaking up, also, the rayles, of which they compiled bonfires; tumbling the communion table over and over. They were, also, so offended with the memorials of the dead, that not one monument in the church remained undefaced, When their unhallowed toylings had made them out of wind, they took breath afresh on two pair of organs, piping with the same about the market-place lascivious jigs, whilst their comrades daunced after them in surplices. The clappers of the bells they sold, with the brasse they had slaied from the grave-stones; nor was any window suffered to remain unshattered, or remarkable place unruined.

It is well worthy of remark, that the outrage at Wells was conducted by the Protestant church of England men, in the time of Edward VI., and that this attack on Peterborough was carried on by the Puritans, another class of Protestants, one century after, on this very church of England, who had Peterborough in possession; 80 that those, who had been the authors of schism, suffered by the very principles they had introduced: for these fanatics seem to have held the surplices of the establishment in as much abhorrence and derision as the others had formerly the vestments of the ancient church which they had plundered and destroyed.

The fact is, the church of England, in its attempt to keep up episcopacy and ancient church government, has too much of the old system about it to suit the levelling and destructive feelings produced by real Protestantism. At the time of the Commonwealth the establishment was overthrown, and is at present in a most insecure state, not from the combinations and cabals of Catholics, but from the extending principles of contempt for ecclesiastical authority, and the all-sufficient private judgment in matters of religion, which are inseparable from Protestant opinions.

The history of this country, since the change of religion, ought to convince the churchmen of this country of the utter impossibility of preserving a national church or unity of creed. The daily extending sects of dissenters are ample evidences of this fact; all of which have been produced by the same principles as those which founded the establishment itself: but, either from inherent hatred against the ancient religion, or from infatuation and blindness, the high church party continually rail against the Catholics of this country as the cause of their decay, unheeding the mass of zealous Protestant dissenters, who openly clamour against them, and the undermining effects of nine-tenths of their own established clergy, who not only disbelieve, but openly condemn, various portions of the articles, creeds, and discipline, as they are at present by law established. For a confirmation of this assertion, see that admirable Letter of Dr. Milner to Dr. Sturges, of Winchester, demonstrating the low church principles to be entirely subversive of the original tenets of the Church of England.

S.

Wherever Vandemerk and Sonoi, both lieutenants to the Prince of Orange, carried their arms, they invariably put to death, in cold blood, all the priests and religious they could lay hands upon, as at Odenard, Ruremond, Dort, Middlebourg, Delft, and Shonoven. - See *Hist. Ref. des Pays Bas*, by the Protestant minister DE BRANT.

Of the horrible barbarities practised by this Sonoi, a copious account is given in *L'Abrégé de l'Histoire de la Hollande*, par M. KENOUX, a Protestant author, who draws a most frightful picture of the barbarities practised on the Catholic peasants of the Low Countries.

The reformation in Scotland began by the murder of Cardinal Beaten, in which Knox was a party; and to which Fox, in his "Acts and Monuments," says, The murderers were actuated by the Spirit of God.

Numberless instances might be cited, to shew the horrible excesses committed by these pretended reformers in the furtherance of their principles.

T.

Such was the detestation, only a few years since, to the bare representation of the cross (a symbol that has been used by Christians from the earliest periods), that, when the small Catholic chapel was erected at Lincoln, a plain cross having been formed in the gable by the omission of some bricks, the then mayor sent a message to the priest, desiring the same to be immediately defaced. To which mandate the worthy pastor replied, that he should by no means do so till the crosses on the cathedral, and other churches, were removed; and owing to this spirited answer the cross was suffered to remain.

U.

To what miserable resources are not the designers of ecclesiastical decoration driven in the present day, when all those exquisite symbols and powerful representations of the sacraments and ceremonies of the Christian church, which formed an inexhaustible source for every class of artists, have been expelled and prohibited, as savouring of superstition - a name applied by modern churchmen to every religious truth that surpasses their own narrow comprehension, and every sacred rite which they find too irksome or expensive.

But, will it be believed, these pretended suppressors of superstition, these revilers of those sacred badges which had distinguished religious worship from the earliest period, fly to pagan rites and heathen worship for emblems to replace those they had so barbarously H rejected! Yes; the sacrifice of rams and heifers is sculptured, in lieu of that of the divine Redeemer sacrificed for the whole world; the images of the pagan priestesses have replaced those of the saints and martyrs, whose zeal and constancy laid the foundation of the great fabric of the Christian church: and, indeed, so infatuated have been the builders of modern preaching-houses in this new system, that, from the winged osiris of the Egyptians to the votive wreaths dedicated to the god Mars, they have adopted all descriptions of ornaments relating to pagan rites, which they have introduced without the slightest consideration of their utter impropriety in the places of worship of any class of Christians. Yet, such is the blind prejudice of the mass of persons in this country, that, while such gross violations of propriety are daily taking place without comment, were anyone to be found bold enough to erect an image of the crucified Redeemer within the walls of one of these edifices, an outcry would be immediately raised that popish idolatry was about to be revived; nor would the zealots cease till the object of offence was removed; and should no appropriate Greek or Roman figure be found to supply its place, a neat king's arms, with some appropriate text, would be thought admirably suitable to fill the vacant space.

This is no false picture; it is what has been repeated again and again. Go from the cathedral to the parochial church, and see if you can find one saintly image, or crucifixion, which has not been mutilated or defaced by the rude hand of the fanatic.

Not only has this mania of employing heathen emblems filled the churches with incongruities, but they are universally employed about the sepulchral monuments of persons professing to be Christians, and of which many have been erected at the expense of a nominally Christian country.

Let any candid person survey the monuments erected, during the last and present century, in those great edifices, St. Paul's and Westminster Abbey, and then pronounce, whether there is one sign or symbol by which he could have supposed that the persons, to whom they are erected, professed the Christian faith. Mars, Mercury, Neptune, Minerva, Apollo, and a host of heathen divinities, are sculptured either receiving the soul of the departed, or assisting him in the achievement of his exploits; and, when he regards the costume of the deceased, he is equally at a loss to distinguish the rank, profession, or the age in which he lived. Statesmen, warriors, and even ecclesiastics, have been alike enveloped in the Roman toga; and thus made to appear, both by costume and attributes, pagans of two thousand years ago.

THE END.

WORKS DESIGNED AND ETCHED BY A. WELBY PUGIN, ARCHITECT

WORKS
DESIGNED AND ETCHED
By A. WELBY PUGIN, Architect.

I.

Designs for Gothic Furniture,
CONSISTING OF TWENTY-FIVE PLATES.
PRICE ONE GUINEA.

II.

Designs for Iron and Brass Work,
IN THE STYLE OF THE FIFTEENTH AND SIXTEENTH CENTURIES;

Consisting of Twenty-five Plates of Locks, Hinges, Bolts, Handles, Fire Dogs, Grates, Railings, Vanes, Lamps, Lectoriums, &c.

PRICE ONE GUINEA.

III.

Designs for Gold and Silver Smiths,
IN THE STYLE OF THE FIFTEENTH AND SIXTEENTH CENTURIES.

Consisting of Twenty-five Plates of Cups, Saltcellars, Epergnes, Flagons, Tankards, Salvers, Sconces, Clocks, Chalices, Crucifixes, Monstrances, Reliquaries, Feretra, &c.

PRICE ONE GUINEA.

As the whole of the above Designs have been composed from the best possible Authorities, collected by the Author during several years' research, both in England and the Continent, he trusts they will prove equally interesting to the Antiquary, as useful to the Architect and Designer.

Published by Messrs. ACKERMANN and Co., 96 Strand: and to be had likewise of JOHN WEALE (late TAYLOR's Architectural Library), 59 High Holborn: and JOHN WILLIAMS, Library of Fine Arts, 10 Charles Street, Soho.

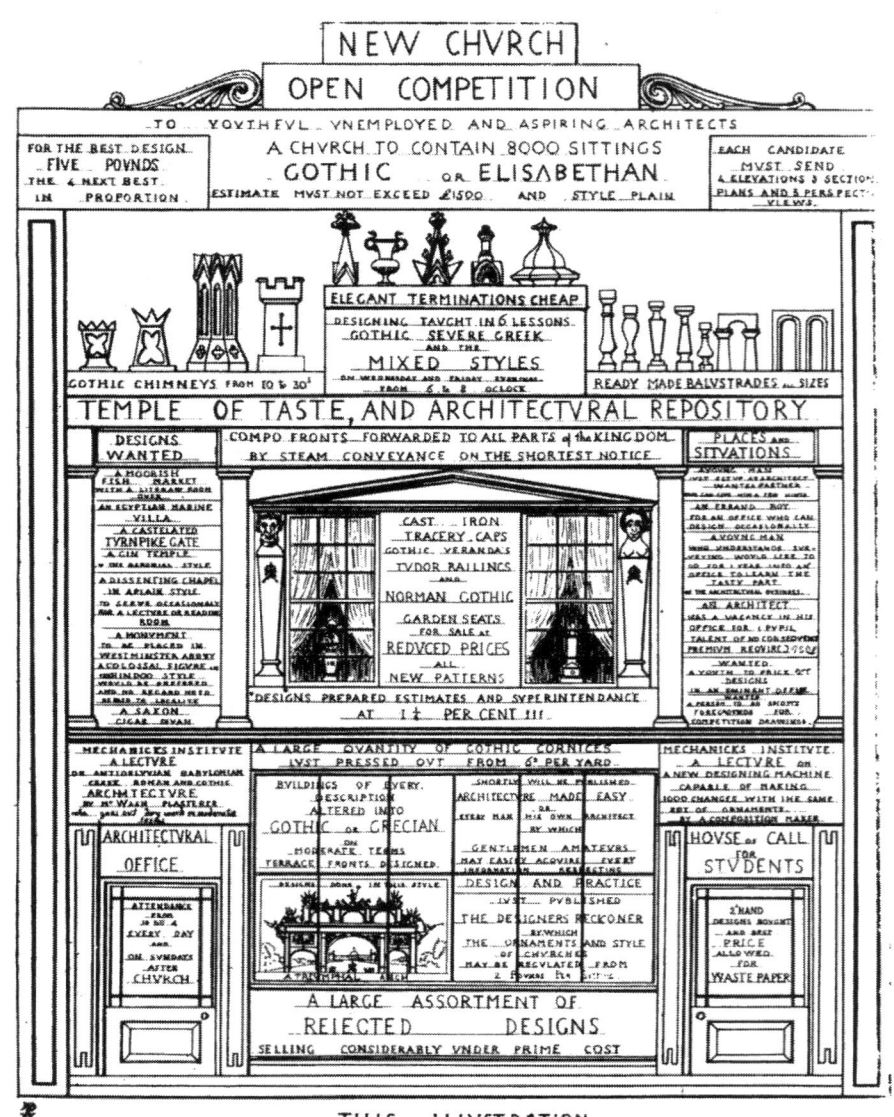

Augustus Welby Northmore Pugin

Contrasts

ST PANCRAS CHAPEL

CONTRASTED CHAPELS

BISHOP SKIRLAWS CHAPEL YORKSHIRE

Contrasts

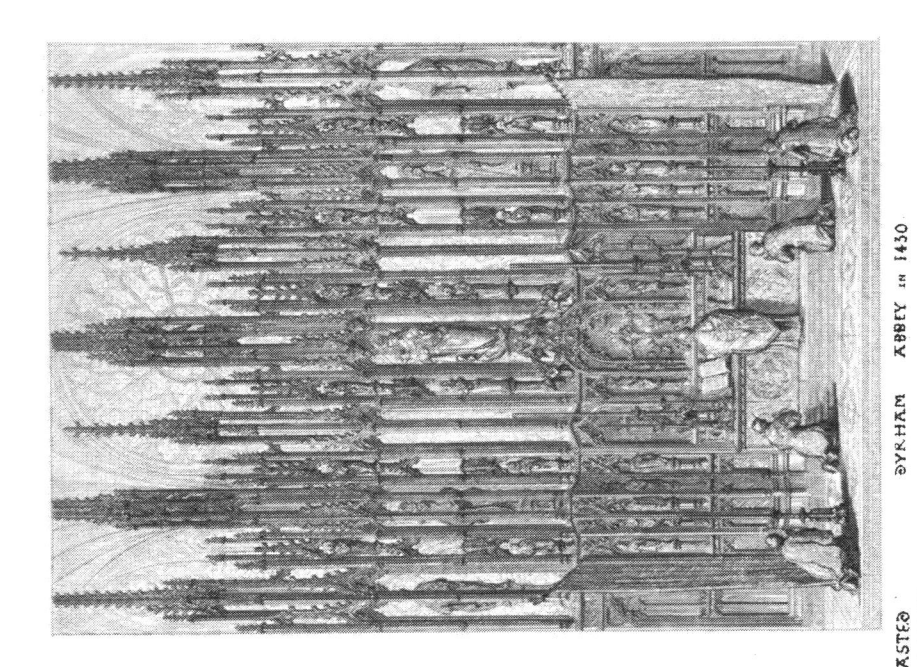

CONTRASTED ALTAR SCREENS

HEREFORD CATHEDRAL 1830

DYRHAM ABBEY in 1430

Augustus Welby Northmore Pugin

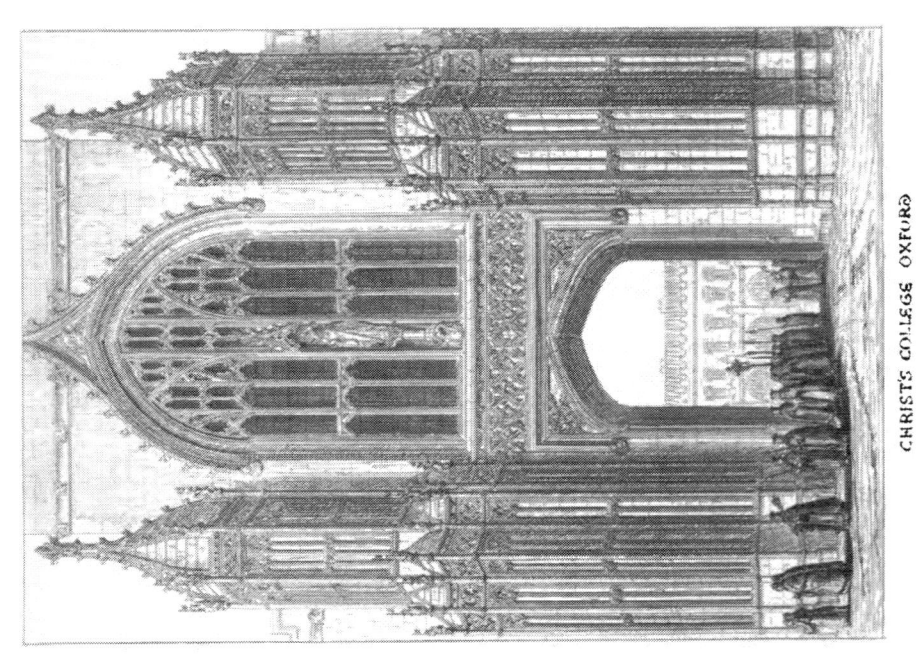

Contrasts

Augustus Welby Northmore Pugin

CONTRASTED CROSSES

CHICHESTER CROSS

KINGS CROSS BATTLE BRIDGE

Contrasts

REFERENCES TO THE
NEW HOVSE.

AAA. THE NVRSERY WINDOWS
B. AN ILL SHAPED MITER
CCC. THE DRAWING ROOM
D. THE STREET DOOR
EE THE PARLOVR
F THE WAY DOWN THE AREA
THIS HOVSE HAS BEEN BVILT WITH DVE
REGARD TO THE MODERN STYLE OF EPISCO-
PAL ESTABLISHMENTS. ALL VSELESS BVILD-
INGS SVCH AS CHAPEL HALL OR LIBRARY
HAVE BEEN OMITTED, AND THE WHOLE
IS ON A SCALE TO COMBINE ECONOMY
WITH ELEGANCE !!!

References to the
Old Palace +

a St Etheldreda's chapel +
b Part of the library +
c The east cloister +
d Lodgings for guests +
e The great hall +
THIS VENERABLE PALACE WAS SOLD
TO THAT EMINENT SVRVEYOR C.COLE
WHO VTTERLY DESTROYED IT AND ON
ITS SCITE ERRECTED THE PRESENT
HANDSOME AND VNIFORM + STREET WITH
ITS NEAT AND APPROPRIATE
IRON GATES IN 1776.
+ brayleys londiniana

ELY HOVSE DOVER STREET
1836

CONTRASTED EPISCOPAL RESIDENCES

ELY PALACE HOLBORN 1536

Augustus Welby Northmore Pugin

Contrasts

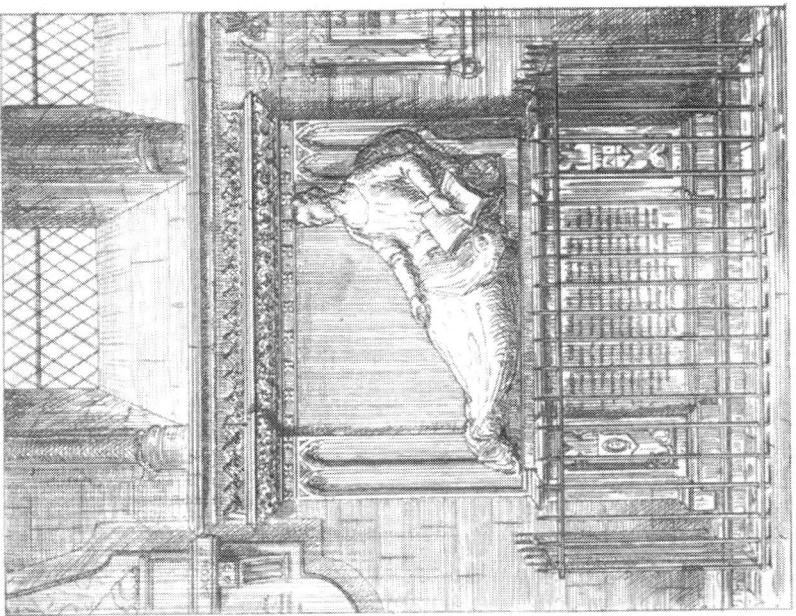

CONTRASTED SEPULCHRAL MONUMENTS

EARL OF MALMSBURY. SALISBURY CATH¹ Chantrey 1823

ADMIRAL GERVASE ALARD. WINCHELSEA CHURCH.

Augustus Welby Northmore Pugin

CONTRASTED TOWN HALLS

HOTEL DE VILLE

GUILDHALL LONDON
George Dance Esq. arch.

Contrasts

Augustus Welby Northmore Pugin

CONTRASTED PUBLIC CONDVITS

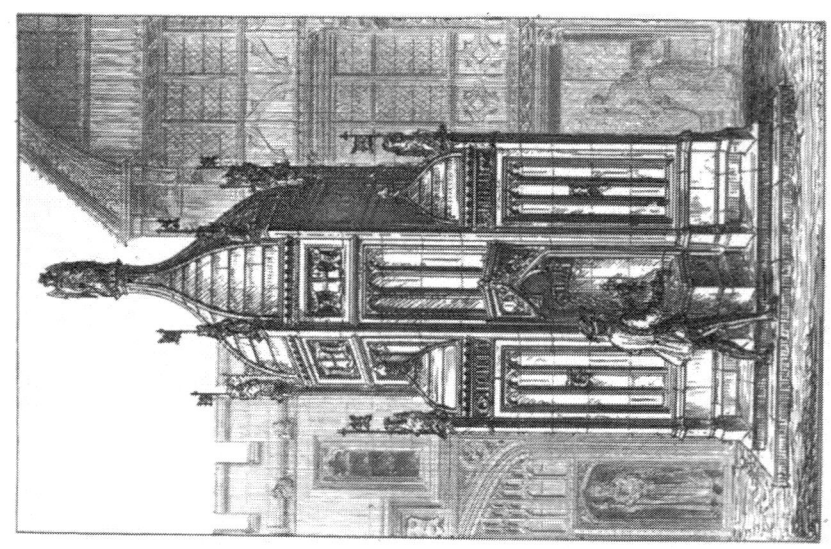

WEST CHEAP CONDVIT
THOMAS ILAM 1479

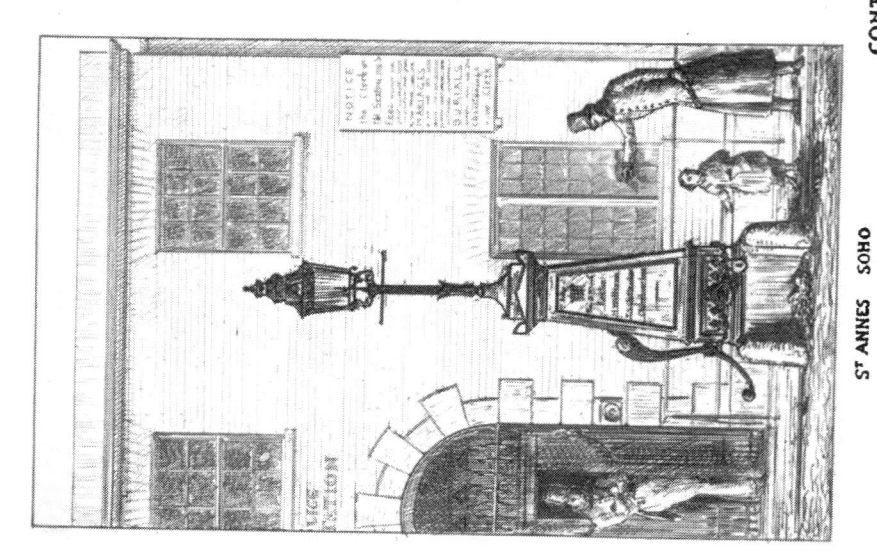

ST ANNES SOHO

Contrasts

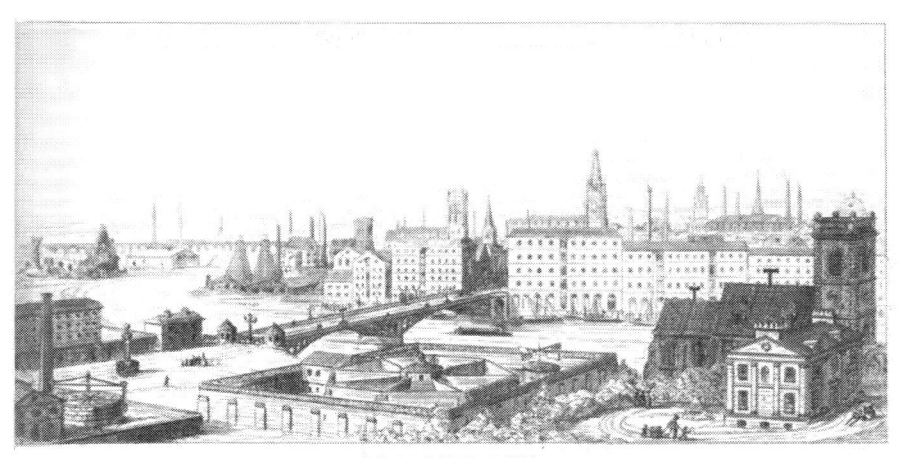

THE SAME TOWN IN 1840

1. St Michael's Tower, rebuilt in 1750. 2. New Parsonage House & Pleasure Grounds. 3. The New Jail. 4. Gas Works. 5. Lunatic Asylum. 6. Iron Works & Ruins of St Maries Abbey. 7. St Evans Chapel. 8. Baptist Chapel. 9. Unitarian Chapel. 10. New Church. 11. New Town Hall & Concert Room. 12. Wesleyan Centenary Chapel. 13. New Christian Society. 14. Quakers Meeting. 15. Socialist Hall of Science.

Catholic town in 1440

ANGEL INN OXFORD

ANGEL INN GRANTHAM
CONTRASTED PVBLIC INNS

Contrasts

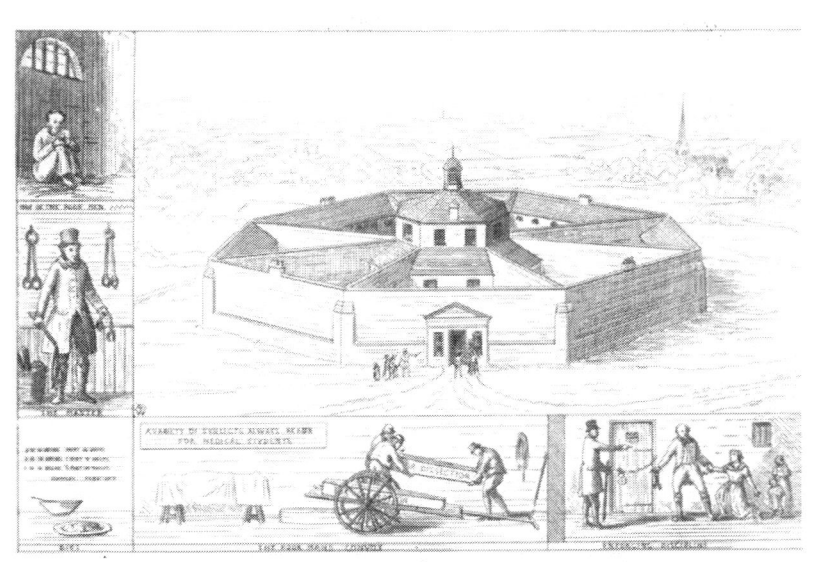

CONTRASTED RESIDENCES FOR THE POOR

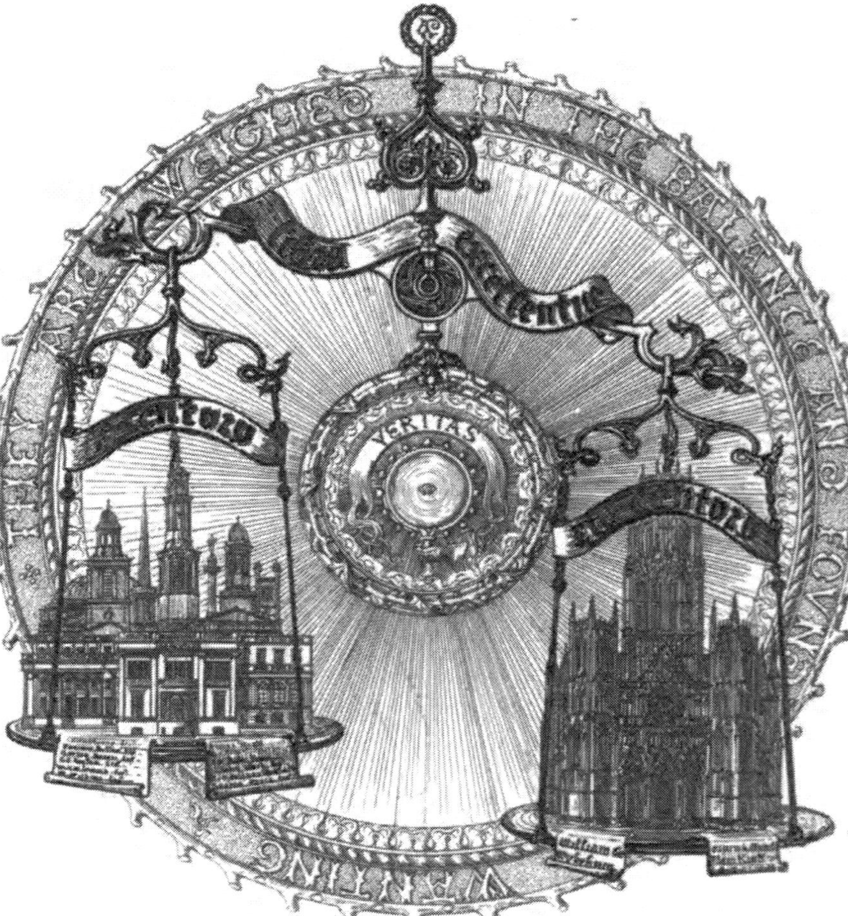
VERITAS

Printed in Great Britain
by Amazon